My Friend Dylan Thomas

Daniel Jones

My Friend
Dylan Thomas

London and Toronto
J. M. Dent & Sons Ltd

First published 1977
Printed in Great Britain by
Biddles Ltd, Guildford, Surrey
for J. M. Dent & Sons Ltd
Aldine House, Albemarle Street, London

This book is set in 11 on 12pt IBM Journal

ISBN 0 460 04314 5

British Library Cataloguing in Publication Data

Jones, Daniel
    My friend Dylan Thomas
    ISBN 0-460-04314-5
    1. Title
    821'.9'12   PR6039.H52Z
    Thomas, Dylan

Contents

Illustrations

For my son Dylan

Preface

It is easier to say what this book is not than what it is. It is not a biography. Events in Dylan Thomas's life are not mentioned simply because they are events in his life, and no attempt has been made to put them into chronological order. Imaginative truth and historical truth are regarded as equal, and I have relied on my memory, without making more than a few references to other sources of information. The book is not a study of Dylan Thomas as a writer. The subject of his work has even been avoided, because it is my view that his work can speak for itself. In this book my aim is to present to the reader the portrait of a character, Dylan Thomas's character, seen from one point of view, my own. The portrait, of course, is not complete, and is seen from an angle, but I hope that the book will at least make a small contribution to a full and true picture of the man, if such a thing is possible.

Swansea, March, 1976

A Winter's Tale

'But he's *nice.*'

It was the day of Dylan's funeral, and his mother was speaking to me in the sitting-room of her home in Laugharne. Her husband, her daughter and her son had died within the space of ten months. I could only try to imagine what she had undergone and how she felt. But outwardly she seemed calm and tranquil; her eyes were clear, her voice gentle, and she looked up at me with a sweet smile.

I was puzzled by her words. I could see many meanings in them, but evidently not the intended meaning. Mrs Thomas had to say again, 'But he's *nice.*' John Ormond, who was standing behind her, helped me to understand. He made a strange gesture, waggled his eyebrows, and winced, at the same time turning pale. Mrs Thomas wanted us to know that Dylan's body was not unsightly, that it showed no traces of decomposition, and that it was ready and decently suitable for viewing. There was a simple pride in her words, and it was impossible to escape a visit to the front room.

The weather had been very fine for several weeks, and when John and I went in, the room was flooded with sunlight. We saw the coffin at once, of course; supported by chairs at the foot of the bookcase, it was a very conspicuous object. In spite of this, a mute, who was present, thought it necessary to indicate its position with an elaborate wave of the hand. He became for me then, and remained afterwards 'the conjurer'.

The coffin was a tawdry thing, covered with some sort of greyish purple embroidery. It was half open, but I could not see

Dylan in it. Instead of Dylan, there lay a grotesque simulacrum of him. My fears vanished at once, replaced by curiosity. I drew near. The American 'morticians' had done a thorough job, true to the traditions described by so many writers from Bret Harte to Evelyn Waugh. In a case like this, use of words like 'face', 'lips', 'cheeks', becomes merely figurative. The whole face was plastered with cosmetics, forehead and skin covered with thick pancake make-up, cheeks heavily rouged, mouth vividly lip-sticked; even the most brassy tart would not have ventured onto the streets in such a get-up. The simulacrum wore a neat executive suit and a bow-tie. The tie was particularly vile. Ruthven Todd had said about it: 'I wouldn't be seen dead in that tie.'

The only sign of life in the coffin was a red carnation, a real one. I knew the story of this. Ebbie Williams and Dylan had made a pact that whichever of them survived would place a red carnation in the other's coffin. Ebbie had not forgotten.

In the meantime, the mute was looking fixedly at me; his eyes held a glint that seemed to combine pride and expectation. There was something I was supposed to do. What was it? Suddenly inspired, I rested one hand on the forehead of the image. I was expecting coldness, but not the cold hardness of stone. After a few seconds, I took my hand away and looked out of the window. What was there to do?

A fly was walking aimlessly up and down the window pane; excited by the unusual warmth of the winter sunshine, it buzzed occasionally. I concentrated on that fly. I thought of the multiple hexagonal facets of the eyes, each tapering to a branch of the optic nerve, the glutinous tongue, the thorax, quickly vibrating and so causing the wings to move, the hairs, covered with dirt, and the abdomen, perhaps full of eggs. Now *here* was something wonderful, something worthy of inspiring awe. But for the rest I could find no interest. However much I reproached myself, I could summon up no feeling for the object at the foot of the bookcase or for anything now connected with it. I was bored. At the same time I was

2

conscious of the mute's gaze fixed on me. Something else was expected now, and on an impulse I nodded slightly.

This was evidently the right thing to do. At once he whisked from behind his back a huge wad of cottonwool and slapped it down not too gently on the face of the image. His action had all the deftness and the expert timing of a conjurer, and the whole performance proclaimed without need of words, 'Thank you for your kind attention: the show is over.'

Outside the room I gave painful thought to the lack of feeling of 'cold fish Jones', as I called myself, and finally decided that this was a kind of numbness, the result of many weeks of too much agonized feeling.

The news of Dylan's grave illness had been announced to me by a journalist in a manner I shall describe later in this book. At that time I knew only that Dylan had collapsed in an American hotel bedroom and was lying gravely ill. Other news reached me with tantalizing slowness. Dylan was in a coma; he was in St Vincent's Hospital, Greenwich Village; no one seemed to know what was the matter with him. I foolishly asked myself whether I could help the doctors in their apparent bafflement. Dylan had been staying with me only two or three weeks before he fell ill, and as far as I could remember he seemed to be in his usual robust health; he was drinking a bit too much, of course, but that was normal. I recalled now that immediately before staying with me, Dylan had taken part in some sort of fracas at a London night-club, and his forehead carried the mark of a bad cut and a bruise where someone, I think, had hit him with a table-lamp. It occurred to me that this might be important. I sent off a cablegram to Dr Gutierrez-Mahoney, the doctor in charge of the case, rather impertinently suggesting some diagnoses, including the obvious diabetes, but adding a detailed account of the forehead injury, with its implication of concussion and brain damage. I don't think I had a reply to that cablegram, but later on I received some kind letters from the doctor, including a copy of the complete post-mortem report.

In the meantime, the news of Dylan's condition continued

3

to be vague. I now sought the help of a journalist friend, Jack Jenkins, whom I asked to telephone Dr Gutierrez-Mahoney on my behalf; I did this because I was unused to transatlantic calls, while he was accustomed to them, and because I felt nervous about the whole business. Jack acted as a kind of interpreter during this three-sided conversation. It remained unsatisfactory until I mentioned Dylan's drinking habits. The doctor had been hedging up to this point, but now his attitude changed completely, and when Jack put down the receiver he was able to give me my first solid piece of information. 'The doctor says that it is to this and *to this alone* that all medical attention is being directed.'

I now consulted my own doctor, a great friend of mine, Charles MacKelvie, and explained the situation. He rang up Dr Gutierrez-Mahoney, while I stood by. A lot of medical phrases I did not understand were exchanged, like 'pial pressure'. When he put down the receiver Charles looked grave; 'They're going to perform tracheotomy,' he said. Then he hesitated, as if he could say more, but he remained silent. Charles was very kind to me at that moment, because he refrained from telling me what he disclosed later on: first, no one had ever been known to survive more than eighteen hours in a deep alcoholic coma; second, Dylan had already been so long in the coma that the oxygen supply to his brain had diminished drastically, causing irreversible damage, with the result that even if he 'recovered' he would be mindless for the rest of his 'life'; third, and therefore, it would be better for Dylan to die.

In the meantime, Dylan's powerful body struggled to hold on to its physical life for the almost unbelievable period of five days. During this time I was subjected to an annoying and irrelevant distraction. I was due to broadcast a piano recital within a week's time; the music was extraordinarily difficult to play, or at least difficult for me, and I had to devote some hours to practice every day, if only to keep my fingers supple. My hands moved mechanically over the keys, while my mind was very far away.

The day before the recital arrived: it was the fifth day of Dylan's coma. I was staying the night with my widowed mother in Cardiff, to be ready for the broadcast there on the following day. Opening the door for me, my mother, a woman of good sense, said without preamble, 'Dylan is dead.'

The news of Dylan's death had strangely different effects on his close friends. Some wept; some became hysterical; some angry; some, suffering from shock, blurted out crazy irrelevancies. One, for example, said: 'What a good thing he just managed to meet Ceri Richards!' As for myself, I became the busy man of action, a part, by the way, that is quite out of character for me. I organized this: I organized that. I appointed myself master of ceremonies, contriver and supervisor of arrangements. My first act was the cancellation of the piano recital and, by permission of the B.B.C., the substitution of a programme of tribute to Dylan. I took part in the programme myself, playing an elegiac composition and reading a short tribute of my own. Before I sat in front of the microphone, I asked for the blind of the control room window to be lowered; the only time I have ever made such a request in a studio. I was no doubt in an emotional state, and I remember thinking my piece, only two hundred words long and written with studied simplicity, 'pretty good'. Now, at a distance of twenty-three years, neither caring for it nor agreeing with a lot of it, I shall spare the reader any quotations.

Then there were the arrangements for receiving Dylan's coffin on this side of the Atlantic. Ebbie Williams, landlord of Brown's Hotel, Laugharne, picked me up in Swansea and drove me to Southampton. On that beautiful early winter day I was in a particularly bad mood, and not even the scenery of the New Forest could change it. I had always found Ebbie irritating, and now he seemed more so than usual. He had the habit of saying the same thing at least a hundred times over, and on that day, referring to the car as 'she', he kept mumbling, 'She's eating up the miles, she's eating up the miles,' and so on.

It was dark when we reached Southampton. At the quayside

I could make out a huge grey bulk, the liner *United States*, lit up in patches by very bright dock lights. It was only then, I think, that I said to myself, 'So it's true.' At one end of the quay, almost hidden from sight, a hearse was waiting.

Shortly after our arrival, a few stewards ran down one of the brightly lit upper gangways; they were carrying paper streamers, coloured ribbons, queer balloons, the remnants of the previous night's Farewell Ball. All were gay, with the prospect of shore-leave and a good time; some of them were wearing paper hats or grotesque masks, some juggled with balloons or blew feather 'teasers' at each other, some sang or played toy instruments, and all made off for the nearest Southampton pub. Lower down the side of the liner, on a dark gangway, men were unloading a shabby-looking box.

My self-appointed role of generalissimo continued on the day of the funeral, and, for some reason, the role seemed to be acknowledged by others. I used Mrs Florence Thomas's house as my 'headquarters' and people 'reported' to me there. Occasionally I went on a 'tour of inspection', usually, of course, to Brown's Hotel. Louis MacNeice warned me that people were trying to break into the hut where Dylan used to work; we walked along to it and found unmistakable signs that this was so, but decided that the stout padlock, having withstood one determined attack, would withstand others. Reports coming in suggested that things were getting wilder and wilder; even out of hand. The day was deteriorating, or improving, according to the way you look at it. Drinkers poured drink not only into themselves but over one another. I was told that Fred Janes was particularly wet on the outside; innocent and sober himself, he had had a tray of six pints of bitter thrown over him, simply, perhaps, because he was innocent and sober. There were some fights and near-fights, in addition to the normal knife fight on the green. Someone suggested that a jar of pickled onions and a pint of bitter should be poured into Dylan's grave. Someone else passed on the news that a certain lady had chosen a singularly conspicuous place

6

where she was making herself available to all comers. A middle-aged roué, with a sports car and an unmistakable glint in his eye, had borne off the youngest of the visitors, a nymphet, barely nubile, on a 'tour of Pembrokeshire'; in reality, of course, to the nearest Carmarthenshire meadow. It was her mother who 'reported' this, calmly adding, 'Whenever there's a wolf around, you'll find that girl firmly clamped in his jaws.'

All these bizarre and grotesque elements, which gradually turned the day of the funeral into a sort of farcical nightmare, seemed singularly appropriate at the time; they were, I suppose, symptoms of a general hysteria, underlying the drinking, the violence, the sex. Even Mrs Florence Thomas's orderly house seemed to be under the influence of a genteel madness of its own. The traditional Welsh ham and home-made cakes were brought out, and we all ate as if we had not eaten for days; scores of cups of tea imperceptibly dovetailed into scores of bottles of beer. Not for the first time, Mrs Thomas read, or had read to her, letters, telegrams and cards from sorrowing relatives and friends. She was particularly proud of this telegram from someone: 'He lived only a short time. But how he lived!'

These words, and the words Mrs Thomas first spoke to me on that winter's day, echoed in my mind at the time strangely, and with more than one meaning. Today, twenty-three years later, I am still asking myself, 'How *did* he live?' and 'But *was* he nice?'

2

Cwmdonkin Drive and School

Swansea is a hilly place. Fifty years ago — not now perhaps — it could have been said that most people had to climb up to or down from their homes. Cwmdonkin Drive, though fairly short, was one of the steepest hills, and Number Five, where Dylan was born and passed most of his early years, stands nearer the top than the bottom. There were no houses opposite the terraced row of the Drive; the green slope opposite was used unsuitably as a sports ground by a private school, Cleveden College, but sometimes sheep were allowed to graze there. The top of the field was divided from Cwmdonkin Terrace by a row of forty-three trees;* I think these were poplars, trees alien to Wales, and even if they were not, they seemed alien, and were sombre in the brightest sunlight. The games, sadly affected by the bias of the hill, were quarrels and fights rather than games. The sheep wheezed and coughed more often than they baa'd, and grazed kneeling. In a city full of gay and beautiful places, it seemed an exceptionally depressing spot, and I had the impression that the atmosphere of the scene out-of-doors managed somehow to penetrate into Number Five itself.

The back room smelt of the self-pity of a despondent schoolmaster; you could usually see a half-finished *Times* crossword puzzle lying on the sagging seat of the armchair where 'D.J.', Dylan's father, brooded away his evening and weekends, when he was not brooding over a glass of stout in the darkest corner of the Uplands Hotel.

The middle room was the room where Dylan and I were

* See *Dylan Thomas: The Poems*, p. 32 and the Note on p. 253.

8

allowed to indulge in our nonsense, provided that we were quiet about it. The light there was very dim, and the gas fire always spluttered, but we easily entertained ourselves and cheered one another up.

The front room, as in so many Welsh houses, was a place apart. I doubt whether any minister of religion ever dared to call on atheistic D.J., but if he had, Mrs Thomas would have received him here. In my time — I shall explain what I mean by this presently — the room was reserved for Nancy, Dylan's sister, older by about eight-and-a-half years, and her long drawn-out 'romance'. I realize now that she was an attractive girl, pursued by a wooer so assiduous and possessive that all other would-be suitors either were discouraged or assumed that she was not free. With no alternative, Nancy took several years to name the happy day.

In my time. I associate Number Five almost exclusively with the earliest period of my friendship with Dylan. After the first year or two, nearly all our meetings were at Warmley, my home. The reasons for this will become clear. In the meantime, it is enough to say that Warmley and Number Five were at opposite poles. For Dylan, Warmley — well named — became more than a second home: it became the home he preferred; and there he formed lasting friendships, with Fred Janes, Tom Warner, and many others.

But it was in Number Five that I saw and heard, though I did not then understand, what went on in the Thomas family. Many years later, I saw and heard more, and had time to try to understand.

Nancy's marriage ended in divorce. She married again and was happy for some years; then she died prematurely, within ten months of her father and her brother. To Nancy, in the Cwmdonkin days, Dylan and I were invisible; we were not even visible enough to be obnoxious. To me, Nancy seemed very attractive, very elegant; ignoring us, she always whirled away, leaving behind an exotic perfume of fur and scent. 'This is my friend's sister,' I told myself sternly, without understanding my feelings or my thoughts. But what really was the relationship between Dylan and Nancy? Outwardly, an armistice of coldness and silence had been agreed. There must have been a faint dislike on both sides; there may have been more. Some of the tales Dylan invented about his sister, unusually malicious even for him, suggested either that he indeed hated her or that he wished me to hate her.

With a brilliant son, an elegant daughter, and a husband whose powers remained mysterious, unrecognized and un-recognizable, Mrs Thomas — Florence — merely sat in at the happy family game. She showed the proper respect a Carmarthenshire farmer's daughter should presumably have for an Aberystwyth graduate, and always timidly called him 'Dad'. Florence was a very kind, sweet woman, and I like to think that most of the qualities that won Dylan all the friends who loved him came from her. She seemed cowed by her position in the family, particularly by the strain of standing between father and son, and whatever sociability she naturally had was repressed. The Thomas family had lived long enough in Cwmdonkin Drive to have made friends with their neighbours, but after so many years, their neighbours remained, at the best, distant acquaintances. When D.J. had to go to London for treatment of a growth on the tongue and Florence had to accompany him, she did not turn to any neighbour but to my mother to ask her to put Dylan up while they were away. During the long period when Dylan spent almost all his time at Warmley and I scarcely ever appeared at Number Five, Florence must have felt a certain awkwardness in the situation. Meeting my mother by accident one day, she made what amounted to an apology: 'Mr Thomas is very nervous, and he has enough to do with boys during the day.' This remark served a double purpose: it explained why I might feel unwelcome at Number Five, and why D.J. completely ignored the existence of my family: he was 'very nervous'.

D.J., senior English master at the Grammar School, made himself and others the victims of a perpetual grudge. The cause of his discontent and self-pity was never put into words, but was explicit in other ways. He considered that his abilities earned him in justice at least an Oxbridge Chair rather than the 'humbler' position of schoolmaster. He despised his profession, regarded his charges as little animals, and looked down upon those who were more or less content to be schoolteachers and tried to be good at the job. He was therefore feared by the boys and shunned by his colleagues. The arrogance of the man needed no words to make itself felt, but occasionally it did find words. Often, after a long thoughtful silence and à propos of nothing that had been said or done, he would announce to the class: 'I have forgotten more than all of you put together will ever know.'

D.J.'s feelings only very rarely exploded into violence, but he had learned over the years how to express irony and supercilious contempt in actions as well as in words; for example, he knew how to knock sarcastically on a classroom door as if for permission to enter. He was neatly dressed and gentle-voiced, but every boy felt that beneath the gentlemanly exterior there seethed a rage only just kept within bounds. I can remember only one instance of physical violence, when, during a reading of Wilfred Owen, a boy, who was probably not listening at all, gave vent to a nervous giggle. D.J., who had had a hard time schoolteaching throughout the '14-18 War, then took it upon himself to avenge the heroic dead by setting us an example of non-violence. We all thought he really was going to kill the boy, but were so terrified that none of us dared to move during the savage beating.

This kind of thing happened rarely, but it is worth mentioning as an example of the tendency to violent righteous indignation which D.J. seems to have passed on to his son. With Dylan, too, there was no warning of an 'attack', and the apparent causes were usually trivial; on the other hand, there often seemed to be hidden behind the wrath some secret feeling of guilt, and this, I felt, was the true cause of the righteous indignation.

11

But it was not by physical violence that D.J. kept the boys in a state of fear and dread. Some of the masters used to slap, punch, or kick us. We didn't mind this in the slightest, and even liked many of them: it was fair, and it was 'school'. But the whip-lash of D.J.'s tongue held us in terror, and most of us had tuned our ears sensitively to his subtle allusions and even to the sarcastic modulations of his voice. He was feared even by his fellow masters, who gave him as wide a berth as their duties would allow.

I have dwelt on D.J.'s character for two reasons. It explains much that seemed contradictory and perverse in Dylan's nature, and it suggests that Dylan's attendance at the school where his father was senior English master was unfortunate in some ways. D.J.'s character had brought about a situation at the school that allowed Dylan complete freedom. He flatly refused to observe discipline, and attended or did not attend classes just as he pleased, recognizing no timetable, sometimes strolling into or out of classes, or into or out of school, according to his whim. No master, of course, dared to punish him, because of the consequences in the staff-room. As a result, Dylan's name, if recorded at all, appeared 'at the bottom' in all subjects except English, and even in English there was no way to contrive to place it much higher than the bottom. Certainly without passing, and perhaps not even trying any examination, Dylan left school as soon as possible. Perhaps it would be nearer the truth to say that there was a transitional period during which no one was quite certain whether he was a pupil or not; then gradually the intervals between his appearances became longer, and finally he appeared no more. His father had found him a job as a reporter on the *Evening Post.*

But Dylan was not a failure in all aspects of school life. Outside academic routine, which he found insufferable, he was good at things in which he was interested, or — and this is nearer the truth — interested in things at which he was good.

Throughout his life, Dylan was very conscious of his height, which was below average. Later, horizontal growth made up for this, but at school his looks were deceptive; the curly-haired, puny-looking boy was in reality very strong indeed. Any bully who thought he had an easy victim in Dylan was due for an unpleasant surprise. Queensberry rules were not observed. To the bully it would seem like attacking a wild cat with bare hands, except that in addition to fearful bites and scratches there would be some well-placed kicks. But private triumph over a bully was not the kind of satisfaction Dylan went out of his way to seek. His moment arrived with every School Sports Day, when spectators packing the field and the grandstands saw with amazement the little curly-headed boy outstripping them all in the three-mile race. Dylan Thomas had won again! — and had won by strength of determination alone, a determination that placed him inexplicably ahead of the brawny boys who lay exhausted beside the track.

But the school play gave Dylan his finest public opportunity. In those days, as if subjected to teetotal propaganda, we were afflicted with a Drinkwater chronicle-play epidemic. Perhaps this was because all the female characters are respectable, and look not too silly when played by boys — that is, not as silly as boys look when wearing beards. I remember Dylan in *Abraham Lincoln* and *Oliver Cromwell* — particularly in *Oliver Cromwell*, perhaps because of the way in which the Wart, not adhesive enough, kept slipping to other parts of his face. In stage movements, gestures, facial expressions and timing, Dylan was no actor; but he never forgot his lines, and always declaimed them, whatever their meaning, loudly and clearly in a rich, though — at that time — rather high-pitched voice. In memory and diction he had no rival among the other boys. His qualities as an actor were duly noted in the School Magazine.

The School Magazine, by the way, was written by Dylan. But this is an exaggeration. During our first term, there was a different editor, and, soon afterwards, Dylan took over. It is an exaggeration, too, to say that he wrote the whole magazine; indeed, he interpreted his editorial duties rather broadly, and the initials D.M.T. are no cast-iron guarantee of authorship. I am not implying that Dylan was a plagiarist; the question of authorship was taken very light-heartedly, and someone else's idea, if good enough, was fair game. Some of my own attempts at poetry appeared in these magazines, together with some of our alternate-line collaborations. One issue contained an essay on 'modern poetry' by Dylan and an essay on 'modern music' by myself. I had been unable to resist the temptation to include in my essay one mythical composer, Dslepp, on whom I expatiated freely — a much easier task than writing about a real composer, and safer, since there was no possibility of error or contradiction. But D.J. smelled a rat. Incidentally, he acted as supervisor of the magazine, and always conferred with his son about it, sometimes in the classroom. It was in a classroom that I overheard the conversation about Dslepp. 'Who's this Dslepp? Never heard of him,' said D.J. Dylan answered with a perfectly straight face, 'Oh, an obscure composer — Croatian, I think.' And Dslepp passed through the censor's net into print.

One of the most remarkable features of Dylan's editorship was the length of his period of office. By special dispensation, it continued after he had apparently left school.

My own relationship with Dylan's father was exceptionally uncomfortable for special reasons. English was my principal subject throughout school, and it was to be the subject I read at University. Not surprisingly, I was singled out for special attention. One example will be enough. D.J. was a fanatical admirer of the novels of George Meredith. I tried hard to read Meredith, but could not then, any more than I can now. With a feeling of guilt and hoping for guidance, I admitted to him: 'I'm sorry, sir; I've really tried, but I simply *can't* read George Meredith.' D.J. adjusted his pince-nez — always a warning of a stiletto-thrust to come. 'I'm not at all surprised, Jones; Meredith is strictly for the Intellectual Man.'

The relationship between D.J. and my family remained negative, even when Dylan was spending all his free time, except for sleep and breakfast, at Warmley. Again, one example will be enough. My father, who was a very sociable and

14

unsophisticated man, once sat opposite D.J. in a tramcar and recognized him from a photograph. 'Excuse me, aren't you Dylan's father?' 'Dylan Thomas? Yes.' 'Oh; well, I'm Dan's father.' 'Indeed?' And D.J. spread *The Times* open between them.

Dylan's relationship with his father was very complex. Even now I am not certain about it, and much that I can say is little more than conjecture. The subject was almost taboo. I felt I could hardly ask Dylan what that relationship was, and he showed no wish to speak about it, perhaps from a sense of loyalty. The situation changed slightly when Dylan was older and his father had retired. When the Thomas family was staying in Witney, Oxfordshire, at a house set in very pleasant country scenery, Dylan told me: 'Father is still as bitter as ever. He got up the other morning and looked through the window to the left, to the right, and straight ahead. He sneered, and, putting every ounce of venom into the words, said, "*Grass! Grass!* everywhere — nothing but *grass!*" '

Dylan's relationship with his father must have been very strained during his schooldays; it is clear that he avoided him both at school and at home. However, it was equally clear that he respected his father and was proud of him, and that any would-be detractor would be wise to remain silent about him in his presence.

The relationship between father and son gradually improved with the years, after the father had retired from his despised profession and the son had given him grandchildren. It would be easy to say that D.J. himself mellowed, but this would be misleading, or at least an over-simplification. He was obviously soothed by Dylan's increasing fame, which softened the cruel outlines of the dreamed-for University Chair that never was. A stranger, meeting D.J. now for the first time, would probably have been deceived by his trembling, courteous gestures and gentle voice. I was not deceived. The indignation had dwindled to self-pity, acidity had become a slight sourness, and the fibre of his rage had dissolved into something liquid, pathetic. I

15

preferred D.J. in the days when he played the part of a well-camouflaged tiger, proud and prowling through a jungle of schoolboys. But this preference may be the result of prejudice on my part; I had known D.J. for too long from the uncomfortable side of a desk.

In the last days, when Dylan's parents lived in Laugharne, at The Pelican — so called because it once had been a pub — Dylan seemed to get on very well with them. He was always a most dutiful son; I stress this because some have suggested that it was not so. Dylan's Laugharne routine was almost invariable, day after day. In the morning he would call at The Pelican, perhaps help his father to complete *The Times* crossword, and then go into one of the many rooms of the fine old Regency terraced house to work. Lunchtime meant for Dylan many pints of beer at Brown's Hotel opposite, followed by work in the Hut, a shed in or near (I never could decide) the garden of the Boat House. Whatever the pressure of work, whenever Dylan was in Laugharne, he saw his parents in their old age for some part of every day.

I feel that I have laid too much stress on the dark side of the father's influence. There is a brighter side. Dylan was brought up in an environment of books and had before him the example of a man who loved literature and chose his words with meticulous care. The library was small but, within its narrow limits, chosen well. There were no foreign books, except a few of the most famous, in translation. There were no books representing English literature before the formation of the modern language, and the emphasis lay heavily on the nineteenth century. Poets established in the twenties were, quite understandably, D.J.'s 'modern poets', and were consequently among Dylan's earliest influences.

Dylan inherited from his father, and learned from him by unconscious imitation, his beautiful speaking voice. That voice, which I still remember, never abandoned its natural pitch. In this, D.J. differed from Dylan, who, when reading poetry,

16

transposed his naturally rather high voice down to its professional pitch, about a major sixth lower. But, underlying Dylan's normal speaking voice, the sounds of his father's could be heard.

It is fortunate for Dylan that he inherited from his father, apart from an irritable sensitivity and the flaming temper of the righteously indignant, only his beautiful voice and love of literature. All the qualities of kindness and delicacy of feeling that have endeared Dylan to his innumerable friends he seems to have inherited from his mother.

3

Warmley

Warmley, my own home, was about ten minutes' walk from Cwmdonkin Drive: a short distance for walking, but by other standards of measurement very distant. Warmley, not Cwmdonkin Drive, became the regular Dylan-Dan meeting-place, and Warmley, not Number Five, became Dylan's real home. There were many reasons for this, and all of them, I hope, will become clear in this chapter.

The family consisted of my father, my mother, her cousin, whom we called Aunt Alice, and my brother Jim, four-and-a-half years older than myself. Dylan immediately became and remained a member of the family: a third son, another brother, another 'nephew'.

Everyone at Warmley was unconventional and easy-going in the extreme, and unselfconsciously so. It didn't matter how much noise or mess we made at any time. Our games, literary or musical, were approved, and sometimes even the older members of the family took part. The house itself, large and semi-detached, offered great advantages. Two of the three sitting-rooms were fairly spacious, and there was an attic occupying the whole house area. Only the back garden was small, but no attempt was made to grow anything there; it was simply a grass plot, large enough to serve as the pitch for a fierce type of cricket.

My father, whom Dylan described as 'the finest type of Welshman', was a romantic in his attitude to every aspect of life. His own creative artistic gift was in composition; he wrote a great quantity of vocal — especially church — music. At the same time, his appreciation of all the arts, without being systematic or particularly well-informed, was wide. His enthusiasms were easily aroused, and once aroused, remained strong. For example, at some time in his youth he had read Flammarion, Fabre and Maeterlinck. A lasting enthusiasm for astronomy and entomology was born. He believed in God, but was anti-clerical; God to him was Nature, and he often said that, instead of sermons, lectures on natural history should be delivered from the pulpit. Bees and Botticelli, Saturn's rings and the Sermon on the Mount, motets and Michelangelo, all were fused in his mind into one romantic glory. In the evenings, instead of writing still more church music, he would sometimes cover sheaves of paper with words. 'What are you writing, Father?' 'I'm preparing a lantern-slide lecture on Religion in Renaissance Painting', or, 'I'm writing an essay — just for myself — on The Harmony of the Universe.' Some of these essays are still with me; they would probably make an expert on any of their subjects shudder, but they cannot be accused of a lack of sincerity and enthusiasm.

My father had an influence upon Dylan that was both subtle, in a way that can be guessed from what I have said, and direct, in a way I shall now try to describe. However strong his other interests were, my father was more deeply interested in human beings than in anything else. He had a personal magic, derived no doubt from that sympathetic interest; even strangers were drawn to confide in him their most intimate secrets on short acquaintance. He attracted adventures; something seemed to happen to him wherever he went, dramatic, humourous, macabre, always extraordinary in some way and almost unbelievable. My father told his stories magnificently, particularly in solo performances at the supper-table, keeping us all in silent suspense or uproarious laughter. He was the funniest man I ever knew, with the possible exception of Dylan himself.

Most of father's stories, of course, had to do with Wales. He had had a busy career as a National and local Eisteddfod adjudicator, and told some hilarious Eisteddfod tales. But the most striking stories were about people he had known in the Welsh countryside, people in little Welsh towns and villages, their characters, what they did, and what happened to them; all of this, characters, comedies, tragedies, were so extraordinary that they seemed almost incredible, but they were all true. Dylan listened; listened, and later remembered.

The rest of my family I can describe much more briefly. Their influence on Dylan was, I think, less direct; they contributed, of course, to the very special atmosphere of Warmley, but they were, perhaps, more in the background, providing a congenial environment.

My brother had musical gifts; he composed a little, and played the piano and the organ. But he was the most remote of the three remaining members of the family as far as we were concerned. This was due to the significant difference in age of four-and-a-half years between the two brothers. Jim sometimes collaborated in a poem or took part in a musical 'aleatory' session, but usually he was 'somewhere else', playing serious cricket or hockey, going to the 'flicks', perhaps taking out a girl.

As for my mother, her singing days were over, but she could still savagely attack Beethoven on the piano keys with her small hands. Her principal creative art was Needlework. This statement is not as modest as it sounds. While most needlework is spelt with a small 'n', hers was with a capital; she had, for example, held a 'one-woman' exhibition of tapestries in London. Perhaps it is worth mentioning as a curiosity that while my father, my brother and I shared the sense of absolute pitch, she had a sense of absolute colour, carrying even the most subtle shade in her memory.

Aunt Alice, my 'second mother', was extraordinarily gifted in the art of teaching. She was perhaps the only teacher I have known who could maintain strict discipline by kindness alone. The word 'governess' sounds silly today, perhaps, but I cannot avoid using it. Aunt Alice was my governess up to the day when I went to the Grammar School. She took this duty very

20

seriously, and from the age of five I had to follow a strict timetable. At eleven, I already had a good grounding in many subjects that were usually introduced to pupils only then, or not till even later. Aunt Alice played the piano fairly well, but was too shy to play before strangers. It was from her that I learned the musical elements and the piano, and in these subjects, for special reasons, she began tuition actually before I was five; the earliest composition I still have, *The Moon*, was written when I was four.

This, I admit, is dangerously near a digression into auto-biography, but I maintain that it aids an understanding of my earliest relationship with Dylan. Can the word 'sophisticated' be used of eleven- or twelve-year-old children? If so, when Dylan and I first met, I was the partner who had by comparison a certain academic sophistication. Dylan was sophisticated in other ways; for example, he boasted to me then that he used to play strip-poker with the maids at M.L.'s house, and, whether this was true or false, the truth or the fiction (which I did not understand) did exist if not in reality, at least in his mind.

The Warmley atmosphere is difficult to convey. The last impression I want to give is that the Warmleyites were smug, arty, and affected. Dylan and I had the same irrepressible energy and inclination for violence as any other boys. We had some desperate fights, indoors and outdoors; they were fearsome, accompanied by savage 'fraps' (our name for blows with stiffened fingers), but lacking any sense of animosity, and divided into proper rounds with breathing spaces. We drank beer together: at first, half-pints of mild at the nearest pubs, sipped shudderingly and made to last as long as possible, then, later, gallons gulped with relish and at speed during pub crawls. We invented boisterous games, many of which ended in destruction. My father's silver-mounted presentation baton was taken from its case and used in a duel until it broke and had to be hidden. 'Where's the baton the LlanX choir gave me?' he wailed, 'I want it to conduct my cantata for the visit of Princess Helena Victoria! Where is it?' No answer. One of the games,

21

which consisted simply of throwing cushions, was revived by us
many years later when we were staying with Roy Campbell.
Imagine trying to put together a broken aquarium in the dead
of night when you've had too much to drink, without waking
your host.

On the other hand, there was an artistic compulsion in the
air, and in ourselves, that led us to play or work of an artistic
kind. The significance of what we did varied from zero to some
degree of serious effort and result. Our most unsuccessful
attempts were in the 'visual arts'. We dug greyish-blue clay from
Swansea Bay, carried it to Warmley in biscuit-tins, washed it,
and tried to mould it. Having found in the garden two boulders
that looked like primitive heads, we took them up to the attic
and tried to make them look less primitive, using chisels and
hammers. The stone was very hard; it simply gave off sparks
and filled the air with the smell of burning. After a week, Dylan
put down his chisel and said, 'I'm fed up with sculpture.' With
pastels and oil paints we turned out work that at least could not
be accused of representationalism; yet, even in its abstract way,
it was plainly unsatisfactory.

Music, or, to use a broader term, sound played a very
important part in our Warmley life. The fact that Dylan had no
knowledge of music or musical skill was much more of an
advantage than a disadvantage, because it ensured that anything we produced in concert would be unconventional; the
results could not be trite, hackneyed, or indeed at all like any
other music. Yet it was not all mere sound-play; by the
workings of chance, interesting effects were bound to occur
and, beyond this, we were sometimes possessed by a mysterious improvisatory power which, leading the way by intuition
shared between us, enabled us to achieve, or imagine we
achieved, a genuine expressiveness. Here, of course, I am
referring to the rare 'heights'. There were levels of all degrees
below these, all the way down to the ground; but even there,
though there was no musical value, what we did was well worth
while as a source of fun.

The instruments of the Warmley orchestra, which were used by any friends who happened to be present, were partly conventional, partly unusual. The piano, two violins (one tuned as for a viola), a 'cello (with a blind cord serving as the C string) and two recorders were the conventional instruments. The percussion section, consisting chiefly of biscuit tins, was large. To complete the ensemble, there was a very old motor horn, in which we managed to puncture a hole; this was capable of producing several very odd and unpredictable notes. To these instruments we sometimes added our voices, at natural or artificial pitches.

A whole mythology of composers, instrumentalists and singers was invented; some of the heroes of this mythology were Max Tonenbach, Paul America, Winter Vaux, X. Q. Xumn, Lacketty Apps, and, above all, the Rev. Percy, who dominated the musical scene with his innumerable piano pieces for four hands. Opera was not forgotten. In this medium the great composer was X. Q. Xumn, whose principal opera, *Blacker Moon*, was so long that only extracts from it could be performed on any one occasion. There were three acts: reasonable enough, it might seem. Yes, but each consisted of four hundred scenes, some of which were complete operas in themselves; one scene in Act Two, for example, consisted of Bizet's *Carmen*. If Xumn was prodigal in music, especially other people's music, he showed remarkable restraint with the words in another of his operas, *Heinrich.* Having said 'Heinrich', I have really said all. The libretto consisted of a repetition of the word 'Heinrich', sung with every possible shade of emotion, from the tragic to the joyful, from the submissive to the peremptory.

In chamber music, every combination of the instruments at our disposal was used, according to the number of players available. Sometimes we arranged events according to a kind of musical pointillism. Each player was allowed only one note, chord, hoot, bang of his instrument at a time, and the 'turns' were regulated according to a strict pre-determined pattern. If,

23

for example, there were six players, the pattern might be ABC DEF ABCABC DEFDEF ABCABCABC DEFDEFDEF ABCABC DEFDEF ABC DEF. These sessions nearly always broke down in laughter, for one reason or another. The sound of a broken note on the motor horn immediately after a bang on the biscuit tin is, I can assure you, mirth-provoking. Funniest of all, perhaps, was the cause of a sudden caesura in the 'music'; we would all gloat at the red-faced embarrassment of the player who had taken a little time to realize that, according to the pattern, he should be playing. There was singing; there was playing; there was also chanting. Dylan and I devised several chanting pieces, half spoken, half sung, sometimes based on words taken at random from the dictionary, sometimes based on nonsense syllables.

Grand Warmley sessions were introduced by properly prepared announcements and programme notes. Here is one of those programmes: '(1) The Rev. Percy will play three piano pieces, *Buzzards at Dinner, Salute to Admiral Beatty,* and *Badgers Beneath My Vest.* (2) Rebecca Mn will give a recital on the Rebmetpes. (3) Locomotive Bowen, the one-eyed cowhand, will give a talk on the Rocking Horse and Varnishing Industry. (4) Zoilreb Pogoho will read his poem *Ffeifokorp.*' The reader may notice in the last item a trick to which I gave the name 'palingram', the reversal of the composers' names Berlioz and Prokofieff, and, earlier, the htnom Rebmetpes is mentioned. This reversal of words was, as a matter of fact, a strange habit of my childhood; it occurred in my speech so often that my parents became worried. 'No, Dan' they would cry, 'not ananab, navarac — caravan, banana!' Many years later, a reader of *Under Milk Wood* might have said, 'No, Dylan, not Llareggub . . .!'

Perhaps this is the place where I should record the last performance of a work by the Rev. Percy. The reader may be surprised to learn that this took place not very long before Dylan's death. Dylan and I were at the time guests of a lady who was rich and a very great lover of 'culture'. Now for the full savouring of the anecdote that is to follow, it is not irrelevant to mention a certain peculiarity of this lady. At one time she had had her ear-lobes pierced, and the job had been done rather poorly. As a result, in order to keep her earrings level she was obliged to go through life with her head at a slight tilt, as if to catch the sound of a distant elfin voice.

Well, one fine summer afternoon Dylan and I found ourselves alone in the spacious drawing-room looking at the grand piano. 'Shall we have a Percy?' asked Dylan. Soon the sounds of a vintage Percy filled the garden through the open windows. In a few moments there appeared through a window the head of our hostess, characteristically inclined. 'What's that called?' she asked, with the utmost seriousness. Dylan hardly looked up from the keys as he replied promptly *'The Voles' March'*. 'Oh . . . how interesting . . .' (this last word spoken *diminuendo*). And she quickly vanished. The poor lady didn't know which was the greater danger: to suffer the exposure of a flaw in her cultural knowledge, or to be the victim of a leg-pull. Retreat was the surest way out, and she took it.

The reader who is well-informed about 'avant-garde' developments in music will be amazed, no doubt, to find a great many of them anticipated in Warmley so long ago. In my account he will find emphasis on improvisation (for example, in the Rev. Percy's piano pieces), the aleatory (in all ensemble pieces), musique concrète (in the percussive use of household implements), the incorporation of large sections of already composed music (*Carmen* in *Blacker Moon*), fragmentation (patterns of single sounds distributed among players), the mixture of speech, song and half speech, especially with nonsense syllables (chanting) and the use of extraordinary titles (*Salute to Admiral Beatty*).*

Much that I have said so far is mere fun. Our literary collaborations, on the other hand, can be described as 'serious play' and have a claim to closer attention.

* Compare the title of a piece by B. van Nostrand played in Rotterdam on the 3 September 1975: *Emergency Plumbers Manual*.

My Friend Dylan Thomas

In poems we always wrote alternate lines, the odd ones for me, the even ones for Dylan, and we made it a strict rule that neither of us should be allowed to interfere with, or criticize the other's contribution. Our pen-name was Walter Bram, a name probably borrowed from Bram Stoker. Bram's poems were sometimes divided into separate collections, with titles like *Voiceless Frolic*. In an article in *Encounter** I describe Bram's style as 'bafflingly inconsistent': 'it is fragile, furious, laconic, massive, delicate, incantatory, cool, flinty, violent, Chinese, Greek, and shocking; one poem may begin "You will be surprised when I remain obdurate", and the next, "I lay under the currant trees and told the beady berries about Jesus".' The most 'beautiful' of the Bram poems are associated with the action of a god-like character ('He') or characters ('They'). Here are some examples:

(1)† He turned his forehead to the trooping air,
      And stood there breathing like a god;
      He had sought them with a slender rod,
      Calling out to them, 'I am Azelea.' He is there
      Who walks upon the clouds with coral eyes;
      They whom he calls upon are many, 'I am Azelea of the loud sun.'
      He stands preparing incense for their feet;
      'I am Azelea.' His call is sweet.

(2)   They followed for seven days
      The youngest shepherd with exotic praise,
      Seeking grass unshepherded,
      Worship-laden where the magic led.
      They followed the shepherd through diverting ways,
      Watching his satyr footsteps as he fled.

(3)   They had come from the Place
      High on the coral hills
      Where the light from the white sea fills
      The soil with ascending grace.

* January 1954.
† Most of the poems had no titles other than the first lines, but this one was called *Azelea*.

And the sound of their Power
Makes motion as steep as the sky,
And the fruits of the great ground lie
Like leaves from a vertical flower.
They had come from the Place;
They had come and had gone again
In a season of delicate rain,
In a smooth ascension of grace.

Fragile 'beauty' was not always Bram's aim. For example, here is a strange war poem:

There are little cannons kneeling
In the sculpture of the night;
There are queues of soldiers wheeling
In the calculated light.
Elementary sky is full of snow;
Little chanting bullets come and go.

Or this, entitled *Chameleon*, which we considered our champion tongue-twister, to be declaimed from the Acropolis by an orator with his mouth full of pebbles, like Demosthenes:

I am still oracular,
Something with a phalanx male,
Down the date-vernacular,
Pedal tail.

Burdened dome of fortunate
Covers me with various, but
Fountains, blessed with little fate,
China cut.

Pyramid of aching air
Flocks with granite wool, and I,
Wedged between their hazard hair,
Ceiling fly.

I am full of cylinder,
Tidal paper on the vein;
Bird is perpendicular;
Twenty pain.

> In my sunset portico
> Psalms of single lunar grope,
> Watch the winter horses grow
> Gamba slope.
>
> I am psychological
> While troubadours of mind are ripe,
> And standard shells of total call:
> Weeping pipe.
>
> Wheels of monks are demistrung,
> But bloom with longer fun,
> While they spin the candle hung;
> Bundle sun.

Dylan and I sometimes combined the aleatory with collaboration in poetry, as in music, by writing out 'hat-poems'. For these, two hats were needed, one for each of us, and the lines were written on strips of paper which were shuffled and drawn out alternately. No adjustment of lines was allowed after the drawing. In this way we composed an enormous poem called *Asia*. Sometimes chance produced striking confrontations of lines, as in the couplet:

> Hurrah! cones for our small meal!
> One per cent of public moth.

Even in this direction, I maintain, we did not reach the totally trivial and insignificant; we were playing, but playing seriously with words. To quote again from my *Encounter* article: 'We had word obsessions: everything at one time was "little" or "white"; and sometimes an adjective became irresistibly funny in almost any connection: "innumerable bananas", "wilful moccasin", "a certain Mrs Prothero". [But] these word games, and even the most facetious of our collaborations, had a serious experimental purpose.'

Our collaborations in other literary forms were not so successful. We never managed to write more than one or two pages of a 'play', though we spent a lot of time discussing eccentric ideas for plays: for example, the idea that with the raising of the curtain a huge magnesium flare should be set off on the stage, blinding the audience for the rest of the performance. Short stories, written in alternate sentences, were a failure: each of us wanted to go in a different direction, and the whole 'narrative' would zigzag in the most perplexing way. In prose, we achieved something only by collaborating in every sentence, trying to outdo one another with crazy suggestions, and somehow, at the risk of overloading and turgidity, managing to combine them all. We planned a complete biography of the Rev. Percy, but succeeded in finishing only the following fragment, which I give here as an example of our collaborated 'prose'.

PERCY DROPPETH

The Rev. Alexander Percy, Master of Topiary, Doctor of Statistics, Bachelor of Chiropody, Master of Music for Mongolia, Lecturer in Mural Insanity and Eurhythmics at the Sebastopol Sea-scouts' Technical College, Past President of the Sculptors' Reform League and the National Society for Prevention, and now President of the Society for the Encouragement of the Export of Medical Wadding and of the Institute for the Protection of very old Herbalists, Founder of the Percy League, and the First Man to Walk from London to Brighton on All Fours. Chief Whip for the Liberal Government in 1863. M.P. for Lundy Island in 1872, present Manager of Dogger Bank, and veteran composer.

His Official Biography
by
OMEGA B. McFROM B.D.,
pigmy chaplain to His Majesty's Fleets,

with the kind collaboration of the Rev. Percy's many friends, including X. Q. Zhumn (sic.), Paul America, Winter Vaux, Elizabeth Hoop, Waldo Carpet, Xmas Pulpit, Rebecca Mn, Leonard Crosbie-Martin, Max Vrodboydya, Nest Edwards, Hermann Joy, S. P. Xavia, and others.

Alexander Percy was found wandering at an early age with his negro mother on an iceberg north of King Edward VII Land in 1831. He was rescued by redskin refugees who had sped from America aboard the gas-driven dinghy *Our Way of Harnessing Homer* and taken by them to Peruvian territory.

My Friend Dylan Thomas

With them Percy became a great favourite and soon learnt their language. In exchange, he taught them how to develop a civic sense, and how to snare, gauge and merit the wilful albatross. Moreover, he acquainted them with the intricacies of fugue and counterpoint and instructed them to play some of the lesser known works of Rameau (to whom his negro mother was distantly related and with whose music she had made him conversant while upon the iceberg) upon harmoniums and hautboys crudely fashioned from the bark of the gum-tree and the leaves of the not too modest acacia.

Percy was a sturdy babe, and soon erected a useful shanty for him and his mother. They lived on Fish which Percy cajoled from the Amazon and conies which he was able to catch by reason of his superior speed and of that already developing spirit of national endeavour which was in future years to gain him the foremost place among British administrators.

Their happy life, however, was soon to come to an end. In 1840 a number of vodka-sodden muzhiks, incensed by the tyranny of the Tsar's imperial sway over their Motherland, and maddened by the genial cries of the three-toed yaks who in that year ravaged the country so extensively, rushed to Peru in search of the Holy Cony, a modern equivalent of the Holy Grail. Their methods, however, differed from those of the knights of Arthur of yore, inasmuch that bombs were used to intimidate the Fabulous Cony into leaving the security of its lair.

Percy's humble dwelling became the object of a fierce attack by the incensed muzhiks, who believed the youthful composer and his negro mother to be secreting The Cony within. Bombs were thrown, but fortunately no fatal injury was sustained by Percy or his negro mother. She, however, lost a leg.

Over the thousand miles to Panama, through the terrible dangers caused by the many and various wild animals frequenting the jungles, Percy and his now crippled parent rode, on the back of an ecru roan rent by a kindly Peruvian who had more than once profited from Percy's extensive knowledge of topiary, then an unknown art in that place. By the by, the Peruvian, through his newly acquired accomplishment, fashioned from the cacti and the pampas-grass growing in front of his cabin, a number of elegant creatures, unknown outside South American mythology, with which he was wont in future years to attract passing dromedaries, take advantage of their momentary torpor, and attack them, baring his carious teeth.

Near the outskirts of Panama the crippled negress was bitten severely

30

and time upon time, invariably upon the nape, by a white, hat-shaped bird. One legged as she was, with mixed feelings and swollen nape, the prey of tsetses, the jibe of the likely jaguar, she nevertheless rode fearlessly on, cheerfully swinging her sole leg in the breeze.

Reach Panama they did. There they were accorded a civic reception, the loyal burghers having heard of their brave attempts to ward off the muzhiks and of the effect of Percy's topiaric erudition upon Miguel y Bradshaw, the roaner of their steed, whose beautiful cactus productions and pampas creations were, even so soon, the main subject of conversation in every Peruvian hutk, or hut.

A monument was erected to the memory of Alexander Percy in the main square of Panama, facing the Civic Buildings and the Hot Dog Saloon.

(Here McFrom's Manuscript breaks off.)

Dylan and I shared, of course, a literary relationship outside our collaborations. This went beyond mere discussion and interchange of books. He read to me every poem he wrote when it was completed, and often at certain stages before completion. I must admit here to being guilty of writing poetry myself at the time, poetry as rich in quantity as it was poor in quality. I read my poems to him, he read his poems to me, and our critical comments were detailed and frank.

This was, of course, in the 'Warmley days'. Later on, the spring of my artificial poetic fountain naturally dried up, and we no longer saw one another almost every day. But Dylan throughout his life kept up this habit of reading to me every poem at whatever stage it happened to be and whenever opportunity arose, in Swansea, Laugharne, London, Oxford — anywhere we happened to be together or to stay together. The last occasion was in October 1953, when he stayed with me in Swansea on his way first to London and then, for the last time, to the United States. He had often read long passages of *Under Milk Wood* to me before, but on this occasion he spoke about his plans for the evening sequence, which he intended to balance the morning sequence in length, and showed me fragments of it, consisting chiefly of ballads given to some of

31

the characters to sing, for example, The Ballad of Bessie Bighead. The evening, too, was to be 'all singing'.

But I must return to Warmley, and, before leaving it, say something about our very special and important 'Broadcasting Corporation'.

The W.B.C. consisted of one studio (the large drawing-room upstairs) and one room for the reception of 'transmissions' (a small sitting-room downstairs). I lack the technical knowledge to explain in detail how it all worked, but — thanks to the ingenuity of Tom Warner — it *did* work. Three loudspeakers in the studio served as microphones; they had their individual characteristics, and we experimented by placing them at different distances, covering them with cloth, standing them inside biscuit tins, and so on. Two hidden wires led downstairs to the radiogram pick-up in the sitting-room and the 'transmission' came, of course, from the radiogram loudspeaker. The station signal was a metronome; this allowed us to leave the studio empty while adjusting the reception.

The inauguration of the W.B.C. was an hilarious occasion; the account of it came to me indirectly through Dylan and Tom, because I was needed in the studio. On that day, when my father was settled comfortably in his armchair beside the radiogram, Dylan asked permission to tune in to some foreign stations. He played with the dials for a while, and then switched on to the W.B.C. studio, where I was already playing the piano. 'Ah! the Waldstein!' cried father, 'turn up the volume.' Dylan did so, and father listened contentedly. I allowed a minute or so to pass before I introduced the first odd chord. This had an effect on my father like an electric shock. 'A mistake! how unusual!' Then I allowed strange thematic contortions to creep gradually into the music, until not a trace of Beethoven was left in the farrago of sound. Father, red in the face, ran to the door of the room and called out, 'Ettie! listen to this! the world has gone mad!' My mother, answering from somewhere in the depths of the house, called back, 'I can hear it too. It's coming from *upstairs.*' My father was delighted with the trick, and still more by the W.B.C., which he threatened to monopolize by taking up more than his share of studio time.

The problem of the station signal was well solved, but the W.B.C. had other problems. Every member wanted to broadcast and to hear himself broadcast — an impossibility in the days before private recordings. Then there was shortage of 'staff'. Usually three of us took part in the 'broadcasts'; this meant an audience of one and a cast of two in, for example, the two-character scenes from *Macbeth, Hamlet*, and *Anthony and Cleopatra*, or in specially written scripts. Nobody — not even Dylan — was skilled enough to succeed in attempts to assume many different voices. Falsetto, for instance, always sounded ridiculous. Disputes about participation were best solved by the designing of complicated miscellaneous programmes, consisting of verse-reading, music, drama, and talks. Actors and audience would rush wildly up or downstairs in the time it took one of us to announce the next item in a calm, level voice.

I have gone into some detail about the W.B.C. because I believe that its significance was far greater than mere fun. The designing of miscellaneous programmes can be dismissed, perhaps, because not one of us later on was concerned professionally with work of this kind. Verse-reading was a different matter. Dylan, of course, could not hear himself 'over the Warmley air', but subsequent critical discussion was detailed and penetrating. Each of us was subjected to strict criticism. Sometimes we studied a single poem simply with the aim of 'putting it over' successfully; each of us attempted a reading, and then had to undergo criticism. The knowledge gained from these attempts and from the critical discussions was to be put to good use by one of us later on. With no essential difference in technique between the W.B.C. studio and a B.B.C. studio, it would not be too much to say that Dylan served his broadcasting apprenticeship at Warmley.

I have already explained that this book is not meant to be a biography of Dylan Thomas, in the usual sense of the word. Dates are avoided, and even description of events that have no more significance than mere happenings. In this chapter, however, it is important to specify time as well as place.

The first term at the Grammar School, for Dylan and for me, was the Winter Term of 1925. I have before me the first of my set of School Magazines, volume 22, number 3, December 1925, signed in boyish handwriting 'D. J. Jones 3A' (the lowest form) with a poem on page 74 signed 'D. M. Thomas 3A'. Since Dylan was born on 27 October 1914, and I was born on 7 December 1912, he was nearly eleven and I was nearly thirteen at the beginning of the term. Our friendship began immediately — certainly in the first week at school, but at first I visited Cwmdonkin Drive. It was in the following year that Dylan became a regular and constant visitor to Warmley, and, with few exceptions, I stopped calling at Cwmdonkin Drive altogether. In the summer of 1934 I graduated from Swansea University College and at the end of that year went to live in London. Dylan stayed on at Cwmdonkin Drive until November 1935, when he, too, moved to London. The Warmley period, then, consisted of the nine years 1926 to 1934 inclusive.

There is hardly any need to stress the importance of those years in a life that extended only from 1914 to 1953, but I would like to mention two things that may not be known to every reader.

The first is about the very beginning of Dylan's professional career. During the summer vacation of 1933 I met Victor Neuberg at his house, The Vine Press, in Steyning. Neuberg, who ran the Poets' Corner in *The Sunday Referee*, was a sort of literary Mrs Wertheim, 'discovering' and encouraging amateur artists. I met Pamela Hansford Johnson there, and, I'm afraid, was rather rude about her poems, which were due to be published in book form as the first volume of Sunday Referee Poets. When I returned to Swansea, I described my experiences to Dylan in satirical terms, and he listened without a word.

About a week later I was surprised to see Dylan's 'That sanity be kept' in the Poets' Corner with Neuberg's favourable comments. This connection led eventually to the publication of the second Sunday Referee volume, *Eighteen Poems* (December 1934).

Finally, the composition of the famous Notebooks falls well within the 'Warmley period': April 1930 to August 1933. The Notebooks are famous, because they provided the store from which Dylan drew most of his poetry right up to the summer of 1941. After this, he wrote comparatively few poems; they were written very slowly indeed, and were of higher quality. On the other hand, the Notebooks mark a time when Dylan's creative impulse was at its most vigorous.

4

Two Letters

It all happened by accident. Twenty years after Dylan's death I was clearing out a cupboard full of old papers when I came upon two letters from Dylan. I had forgotten all about them. The second of these was very long and, it seemed to me, very significant. The discovery of the second letter was the proximate cause of the writing of this book.

For twenty years I had been under pressure from outside and from inside to write about Dylan. During that period much was written and spoken about him, much that was relevant, enlightening, even perspicacious, no doubt, but also a great deal that was false or misleading. Pressure came from outside in the form of admonitions from friends, or, worse still, a heavy silence of expectancy or reproach. I myself felt that I should correct what I knew to be wrong, and was aware that my testimony to the truth, however narrow in its limitations, could not be given by any other witness.

Against this pressure I opposed a stubborn resistance, stubborn to the extent of a twenty-year fight. One reason for my resistance is easy to express. I was too proud to take advantage of the accident that had made me a close friend of a man who had become so famous. The other reason, a psychological one, is more difficult to put into words. I gradually developed a blockage or a complex about Dylan; I don't know which is the right word to use, but perhaps both words are applicable. The mention of Dylan's name to me by a stranger required from me the greatest self-control, not merely in order to remain calm and courteous, but to avoid making a scene that would be, to him, quite incomprehensible. The actual persecution, and the sense of persecution, grew, of course, with the growth of Dylan's fame; I shall speak of this in a later chapter. Another cause of my resistance was the pain involved in exploring certain areas of my memory.

> Nessun maggior dolore,
> Che ricordarsi del tempo felice
> Nella miseria.

The two letters, unpublished till now, are given here out of chronological order. I cannot remember whether I answered either of them; it is more probable that Dylan and I met soon after their delivery and talked about them.

(1)   The envelope is marked '*oh so urgent*', and Fred Janes has evidently filled in my London address after my name. The letter is written on the kind of sheet that is often included in a pad of writing paper, that is, with very black guiding lines; for this reason: 'on this most significant notepaper'. The previous letter Dylan refers to is given second in this chapter. 'Musical Biscuit of the Year': Dylan means The Mendelssohn Travelling Scholarship, which I had won. Tom is Tom Warner, who was learning the French horn at Kneller Hall.

5 Cwmdonkin Drive.
6.2.36.

RA. On this most significant notepaper I write to Warmley's Bigwig for the first time since August 1935. There wasn't any need for me to write and say 'Ra, Maestro' when you carried off the Musical Biscuit of the Year, because you knew I wasn't exactly displeased about it. I'm coming up to London on Monday (the 10th). How do I get hold of you? Write quickly and tell me. We must meet (we most certainly must meet. There are 350 things I want to tell you). Tom is here with me at the moment, cutting a horn lesson to make 3/- illegally. Can't write. Notes between Warmlies are barmy. Great Men (and the whole point is, of course, that we mean it) must *meet*. And soon. Don't forget. Write before Monday. Love,
Dylan.

37

(2)   The envelope, completed in Fred Janes's handwriting, is unstamped, and evidently has not passed through the post. This suggests to me that Fred found an opportunity to hand me the letter in person; at this time he was sharing a flat with some other artists in Kensington. On the other hand, he often returned to Swansea, especially in summer-time, and may have written me a covering letter, sending both his letter and Dylan's to me in another envelope. I can't remember whether the delivery happened in one way or the other.

Dylan had stayed with me in Harrow earlier in the summer of 1935, afterwards going first to Swansea and then to Ireland. He had evidently mislaid or forgotten the Harrow address.

The irritating number of footnotes is, I'm afraid, essential to an understanding of the text.

Tuesday, August 14 1935.
Addressed, unavoidably, to Fred.

And to be read either late at night
    or when at least *half* tipsy.

Glen Lough
Meenacross
nr. Glencolumkille
Lifford
Co. Donegal
Irish Free State.[1]

This is the first long letter I've ever written to you. I'm not much good at writing letters, I can't strike the, if I may coin a phrase, happy medium between trying to be funny, not trying to be funny, and trying not to be funny. I can't write as I talk — thank God I can't talk as I write, either — and I get highflown and flyblown and highblown and flyfaultin[2] if I try very consciously not to be self-conscious. Take me as I come — sounds like Onan — and remember the dear dead days that had to have a gallon or two of nonsense (often awfully good nonsense) or parch. This is written for two main reasons: first, because I've been socially rude, (*you* can't talk), and Goat has probably shown her horns and Bear has growled and the

[1] Geoffrey Grigson knew of this cottage, which had belonged to the American artist Rockwell Kent, and took Dylan there. Grigson had to leave in about a fortnight, and Dylan remained alone for the rest of the summer, producing a great deal of work (including much of 'Altarwise by owllight') which eventually appeared in *Twenty-five Poems*.
[2] Flyfaultin: either a slip of the pen for 'flyfalutin', or intended.

jealous Hook been as haughty as wadding ever since I said, 'Yes, ten o'clock outside the Queen's Hall,' and then, doom on my roving scrotum, found a Jewess with thighs like boiled string and got drunk and woke up with a headache and a halfpenny and a button.[1] It was, if I may coin a phrase, the same old story. You, I know, don't care a seal or a fig when I flouted (that's a word I haven't used for years, have you?) the conventions and didn't even apologise. My excuse for not apologising is that you're so hard to get hold of, Harrow's will-of-the-wisp, Pinner's Sibelius (I'm still the Swan of Tawe).[2] Give what is proper to give, anyway, to Goat and Hook and Bear, and tell Jumbo, 'There is an india-rubber police-force in Archix.'[3] Make up what story you can to explain my sins away: they won't believe it; on the last morning-after, Bear said 'whisky' in a clear voice, and then leered. The second, and the most important reason for my writing is: I never can believe that the Warmley days are over — ('just a song at twilight when the lights Marlowe and the Flecker Beddoes Bailey Donne and Poe')[4] — that there should be no more twittering, no more nose-on-the-window pressing and howling at the streets, no more walks with vampire cries, and standing over the world, no more holding-the-writing-table for the longest, and wrong adjectives; I can't believe that Percy, who droppeth gently,[5] can have dropped out of the world, that the

---

[1] Fanciful names for members of my family, appropriate to their appearances rather than to their characters — names accepted by both of us. Goat: my mother. Bear: my father. Hook: Aunt Alice. (See 'The Fight' in *Portrait of the Artist as a Young Dog*.) The incident evidently refers to a 'black' Dylan put up while he was staying with us. He not only failed to keep an appointment, but probably did not turn up all night, to the disapproval of my family.

[2] The 'Swan of Tawe' combines at least two allusions: in addition to the obvious one, there is a reference to Sibelius's *Swan of Tuonela*. Dylan may also have known that Henry Vaughan was 'the Swan of Usk'.

[3] Jumbo: the fanciful and generally accepted name for my elder brother, Jim. His imaginative inventions, spoken or written, were quite as fantastic as ours. It was he who invented Archix, a land where anything might, and often did happen.

[4] '*Just a song at twilight*
When the lights are low,
And the flickering shadows
Softly come and go.'

[5] 'Hold-a-writing-table' for the longest: one of our competitive games; the 'player' had to hold an article clear of the floor, using his legs only. 'Wrong adjectives': this feature of our word-games and collaborations, and Percy, chief character of our fantasy-world and symbol of it, have already been described in the chapter on Warmley. 'Percy droppeth': title of his biography (cf. Merchant of Venice IV. i).

My Friend Dylan Thomas

'Badger Beneath My Vest' and 'Homage to Admiral Beatty' are a song and a boat of the past; that Miguel-y-Bradshaw, Waldo Carpet, Xmas Pulpit, Paul America, Winter Vaux, Tonenbach, and Bram, all that miscellaneous colony of geniuses, our little men, can have died on us; that the one-legged grandmother — remember the panama-hat-shaped birds, from the Suez canal, who pecked at her atlas-bone — doesn't still take photographs of Birmingham; that the queer, Swansea world, a world, thank Christ that was self-sufficient, can't stand on its bow legs in a smoky city full of snobs and quacks.[1] I'm surer of nothing than that that world, Percy's world in Warmley, was, and still is, the only one that has any claims to permanence; I mean that this long, out-of-doored world isn't much good really, that it's only the setting, is only supposed to be the setting, for a world of your own — in our cases, a world of our own — from which we can interpret nearly everything that's worth. And the only world worth is the world of our own that has its independent people, people like Percy, so much, much more real than your father or my mother, places and things and qualities and standards, and symbols much bigger than the exterior solidities, all of its own. Didn't we work better, weren't poems and music better, weren't we happier in being unhappy, out of that world, than in — not even out of — this unlocal, uncentral world where the pubs are bad and the people are sly and the only places to go are the places to go to? I think it is the same with you, though it's so long since I've seen you, dry months, too, that you may be, though you couldn't be, all different, all older, in your cat's lights more learned, even Harrowed to some sort of contentment, never regretting for one moment the almost-going of Percy's celestial circle. No, that couldn't be; that world *does* remain, in spite of London, the Academy,[2] and a tuppeny, half-highbrow success.[3] I never thought that localities meant so much, nor the genius of places, nor anything like that. I thought that the soul went round like a Gladstone bag, never caring a damn for any particular station-rack or hotel-cloakroom; that gestures and genius made the same gestures in Cockett and Cockfosters;[4] didn't we look at our geniuses and say, 'We're taking you somewhere else to live, but we won't part.' I placed my hand upon my heart and said that we would never part; I wonder what I would have said

---

[1] 'Smoky city': almost throughout, Dylan is alluding to London (not to Ireland) in contrasting the Warmley and the non-Warmley worlds.
[2] I was at that time studying at the Royal Academy of Music.
[3] Dylan is probably referring to the favourable reception of his *Eighteen Poems*.
[4] Swansea and London districts.

had I placed it on my head. So on and on; like an unborn child in the city I want to get born and go to the outskirts. Here in Ireland I'm further away than ever from the permanent world, the one real world in a house or a room, very much peopled, with the exterior, wrong world — wrong because it's never understood out of the interior world — looking in through the windows. This sort of nostalgia isn't escapist by any means, you know that; just as the only politics for a conscientious artist — that's you and me — must be left-wing under a right-wing government, communist *under* capitalism, so the only world for that WARMDAN-DYLANLEY-MAN must be the WARMDANDYLANLEY-WORLD under the world-of-the-others. How could it be escapism? It's the only contact there is between yourself and yourselves, what's social in you and what isn't — though, God knows, I could shake Bram's intangible hand as seriously as the hand of Dean Inge, and with far greater sense of reality. Even surrealism, which seemed to have hopes and promise, preaches the decay of reality and the importance, and eventual dominance, (I don't like those words however much I try to look on them coldly), of unreality, as though the two could be put into two boxes: isn't Percy flesh, bone, and blood, isn't Evangeline Booth a shadow, isn't Percy a shadow, isn't Evangeline flesh, bone and blood, isn't Percy flesh-bone-and blood-shadow, isn't Evangeline flesh-bone- and blood-shadow, isn't Percy-Evangeline flesh bone and blood? — and so on and so on. I'm not going to read this letter over afterwards to see what it reads like; let it go on, that's all; you don't mind the dashes and the hyphens and the bits of dogma and the brackets and the bits of dog-eaten self-consciousness and the sentimentality because I'm writing this by candle-light all alone in a cottage facing the Atlantic. From the WARMDANDYLANLEY-WORLD I'd no more think of writing this letter than of using words like 'Proust' and 'flounce' and 'akimbo' and 'schedule' and 'urge' when talking in that W-W; I wouldn't have or need to; this is only covering old ground in words and phrases and thoughts and idioms that are all part of that world; it's only because, now, here in this terribly out-of-the-way and lonely place, I feel the need for that world, the necessity for its going on, and the fear that it might be dying to you, that I'm trying to resurrect my bit of it, and make you realise again what you realise already: the importance of that world because it's the only one, the importance of us, too, and the fact that our poems and music won't and can't be anything without it. Soon I'm going out for a walk in the dark by myself; that'll make me as happy as hell; I'll think of the almost-but-never-going-gone, and remember the cries of the Bulgarian scouts[1] as I hear that damn sea rolling, and remember the first world — where do they pretend it is, Waunarlwyd?[2] — as I stand under an absurdly high hill — much too high, our world has its hills just the proper, the *nice* length (I'm arching my index-finger and thumb and joining them tastefully) — and shout to it, 'Go on, you big shit, WARMDANDYLANLEY-WORLD has a hill twice as beautiful and with a ribbon and a bell on it, and a piece of boiled string on the top, if the WARMDANDYLANLEY-MAN wants it like that.' And I'll finish this when I come back.

But it was so late when I came back that I padlocked out the wild Irish night, looked through the window and saw Count Antigarlic,[3] a strange Hungarian gentleman who has been scraping an acquaintance (take that literally) with me lately, coming down the hill in a cloak lined with spiders, and, suddenly very frightened, I hurried to bed. This is written in the cold of the next morning, the Count is nowhere to be seen, and it is only the thin mouth-print of blood on the window-pane, and the dry mouse on the sill, that brings the night back. It's hard to pick up the night threads; they lead, quite impossibly, into the socket of a one-eyed woman, the rectums of crucified sparrows, the tunnels of coloured badgers reading morbid literature in the dark, and very small bulls, the size of thimbles, mooing in a clavichord. At least, they lead to absurd things. Where was I last night? Feeding my father with hay? Offering Hook a newt in a bluebag? I was talking about worlds. We must, when our affairs are settled, when music and poetry are arranged so that we can still live, love, and drink beer, go back to Uplands or Sketty[4] and found there, for good and for all, a permanent colony; living there until we are old gentlemen, with occasional visits to London and Paris, we shall lead the lives of small-town anti-society, and entertain any of the other members of the WARMDANDYLANLEY-WORLD who happen to visit the town; Fred will be a greengrocer, painting over his shop, Tom an armyman with many holidays, Thornley a nearby vicar, Trick a nearby grocer, Stevens a bankmanager with holidays, Smart a bankmanager with holidays, and the

---

[1] Bulgarian scouts: in our fantasy, these cries were produced by playing my 'cello on the wrong side of the bridge.
[2] Waunarlwyd: near Swansea.
[3] Antigarlic: a count of the same type as Dracula.
[4] Swansea districts.

rest of our vague WARMLIES this and that all over the wrong world.[1]
Mumbles, and the best saloon bars in Britain, will be open for us all night.
And Percy will come drooping slow there. Yeats never moves out of his
own town in Galway, Sibelius never out of Helsingfors. So Jones and
Thomas, that well known firm of family provisioners, shall not move out
of their old town. So be it.

But now of course all the things are different; we must pack on and
snoot away in an unlovely city until we can manage our own fates to a
Walesward advantage. If you and the menagerie[2] stay on in Harrow, I
shall, in the winter, come and lodge near there, too, and go up to town
only once or twice a week. We shall twitter. That, at least, is practicable.
And Harrow, hell with such a nice name, shall shine like a star, and the
maidenheads fall like rain.

I am working hard here, and have got lots of new poems. I want you to
see them, I want you to tell me a lot about them before my new book
comes out at Christmas.[3]

Write before I leave here on the thirtieth of August, a long, careless
letter.

All the love of one WARMDANDYLANLEY-MAN to the other one.

This letter marks an important stage in Dylan's life. When he
returned from Ireland, friends noticed a change in him.[*] He
had changed physically, and part of the physical change, in
superficial appearance, was easy to describe; the expressions of
the face and eyes, perhaps, not so easy to notice or to comment
upon. As for the change in his character and outlook it may not
have been observed, but it was there. Then there was the course
of events of Dylan's life, events of the kind recorded by

---

[1] The father of Alfred Janes, the painter, was a greengrocer. Tom Warner, the
composer, was at this time studying the horn at Kneller Hall with the intention
(which he did not achieve before the war) of entering the army. Thornley Jones,
the composer. Bert Trick, who had a temporary influence on Dylan's political
views, was a grocer. Alan Stevens, more a friend of mine than of Dylan's, had just
begun his banking career in Horsham; it was with him that I first met Victor
Neuberg at Steyning. P. E. Smart, writer of many short stories during our
schooldays, also went in for banking.
[2] The menagerie: that is, the members of my family, who had been given fanciful
animal names.
[3] The new book (*Twenty-five Poems*) did not come out until 10 September 1936.
[*] See Constantine FitzGibbon: *The Life of Dylan Thomas* pp. 190 ff.

orthodox biographers. Up to the point when Dylan went to Ireland, this course continued steadily in one direction, and in Ireland the position was static. On his return from Ireland he was confronted by a series of events that swept him, or (as he himself would say) outwardly seemed to sweep him in a different direction.

According to a superficial reading of the letter, Dylan was simply nostaligic and sentimental about the Warmley days, which were over. But, while acknowledging the nostalgia and the sentimentality, he says firmly that this is not escapism, and insists that Warmley is a world, not a locality, or, if it is a locality, localities are much more significant than we imagine. This leads to the core of the letter, which is probably unique in Dylan's writing, because it consists of a serious, direct and unaffected approach in prose to a philosophical question. That question is no less than the fundamental one: what is reality? Is it the fantasy 'inside', or the appearance 'outside', generally observed and acknowledged? Dylan's answer would please some metaphysicians, but few psychologists. To him, the internal is the only reality, or, if there is any reality apart from the internal, its reality is of comparatively negligible degree, and certainly of less significance. The inner world was 'much more real' and 'much more worth while'; 'symbols are much bigger than exterior solidities'.

Dylan had no academic knowledge of philosophy, and up to this point he is following an independent line of reasoning of his own, however familiar his conclusions may seem to some of us. Here, however, he passes into an area of interest to psychologists. The outer world, he says, is 'only the setting for a world of your own'; the artist — he means himself — should inhabit a secret inner world 'under the world-of-the-others'. This was a declaration of intention, and this is what he did.

Dylan became an onlooker, however hard and fast he played an outward part. Whatever it was that had been in harmony with every part of him to form a complete person before his visit to Ireland, from that time withdrew to a place where it was kept hidden and in suspense. I ask the reader to examine any photograph of Dylan taken after 1935. Pose, gesture, action, all the details a cursory glance will reveal, mean one thing; the face, and especially the eyes, mean another. Is it only by hindsight that doom can be read there?

The essential part of Dylan, I believe, was enclosed in a shell, and the desire for freedom, impossible to fulfil, was his personal tragedy.

'Like an unborn child I want to get born.'

5

Dylan and . . .

And games, health, courage, women, drink

In spite of his keen interest in cricket and his early successes in long-distance running, Dylan was not a notable sportsman, either in skill, or, to be frank, in sportsmanship. While he lived at Manresa Road during the war, he acquired a reputation for shove-ha'penny in the local Chelsea pubs; I had a few games with him myself, but the fact that I always lost throws no light on this important point, since I was hopeless. Among sedentary games his favourites were the least skilful gambling card-games; he knew no chess, and his temperament did not fit him for it. For word games involving spelling, knowledge or cryptographic skill, with the exception of an occasional crossword puzzle, Dylan showed surprisingly little interest; they were profitless. On one occasion, when I was staying at the Boat House, I tried to introduce him to an anagramming game with Lexicon cards; I was foolishly proud of having invented it. But after two defeats, Dylan swept the cards from the table, crying, 'A stupid waste of time!'

But the general rule that Dylan was not interested in any game that failed to offer almost the certainty of winning had one important exception: cricket. His lifelong enthusiasm for cricket was not dependent upon personal success. As a spectator, he cared little where he stood to watch the match, whether in the pavilion behind the bowler's arm or in the beer-tent at right angles to the pitch, provided that there was refreshment at hand. As a player, Dylan combined the extremes of aggression and passiveness. His bowling was of the coconut-shy variety, as fast as possible straight at the head of the batsman: cricket *ad hominem.* In Warmley's back garden, our thirty-foot-long 'pitch', I was lucky to deflect these deliveries without damage to spectacles or windows; at least I knew where to expect the ball. Dylan's stance at the wicket was extraordinary: both legs immovably in front of the wicket, and the bat between. There was no L.B.W. rule in Warmley, but it was easy to bowl him round his legs with spinners.

If the reader thinks that I have given too much space to a triviality, I beg to disagree. This is yet another example of Dylan's procedure, conscious or unconscious, in directing his life straight towards its goal, avoiding areas of uncertainty or possible failure, for example, unrelated study, wasted effort or even profitless relaxation, to take the narrow, the sure path.

Dylan was one of the healthiest men and, for his size, one of the strongest I have ever known. His appearance, as a slim, delicate-looking, curly-headed angel in the early years or as a bloated balding cherub in the later, taken together with the morose or dramatic remarks he occasionally let fall, often deceived those who didn't know him well. At first, the talk was all of that 'romantic' disease, so appropriate for the sensitive poet, T.B. The supporting evidence for this claim consisted of a cough (smoker's) and alleged blood-staining of handkerchiefs (shown only once to me), with the despondent prediction, only too tragically true, 'I shall never see fifty'. On the one exceptional occasion, when I was shown a small stain of blood, in my ignorance I became alarmed, and one evening at the Fitzroy, when I was having a drink with G., unofficial doctor of the Fitzrovians, I mentioned the matter. 'Had he been coughing?' 'Yes.' 'Strain. Ruptured small blood vessel. Nothing.' And after a pitying look at me, G. returned to his bitter.

Dylan's liver was subjected to the same occasional upsets most of us experience; but on one occasion, when he spent a few days in hospital suffering from severe depression, the liver was found to be slightly enlarged. On the other hand, as I know from Dylan's post-mortem report, there was no cirrhosis, and, as far as circulation was concerned, no more atheroma (a condition narrowing the arterial lumina) than could be expected from the living through of thirty-nine rather self-indulgent years. With eyes and ears perfect, heart and lungs good, Dylan's physical condition throughout most of his life might have been envied by many people.

My account of Dylan's physical condition raises two questions: his absence from the services in the last war, and the circumstances of his death. The first I shall discuss now, the second later.

Dylan told me that he was called to more than one – he didn't say how many – medical examinations in Llandeilo, and was finally classified as C.3. I saw no documents, and can repeat only what he told me, without guaranteeing that this agrees with any other account. On the other hand, I can see no reason to disbelieve Dylan, since he gave an explanation acceptable to me. It seems that on every occasion when he was summoned to appear for medical examination, he turned up in a very drunken state, and finally was awarded his C.3. When I was in the army myself, I knew a case of a man who was discharged for incurable, habitual drunkenness; he was a liability, and the same logic that brought about his dismissal would, I think, apply to the question of admitting such a man to the forces. As it was, Dylan spent much of the wartime in London, where things were so often scarcely more pleasant for the non-combatant than for the combatant.

Was Dylan a physical coward? Certainly not. He dreaded and avoided pain, but actually sought – especially when drunk – a confrontation with injury or danger. The key to this was the consciousness of his short stature. When he was a boy, he could not resist the challenge of a 'dare'. Someone, for example, once challenged him to cycle all the way down Constitution Hill, a cobbled street so amazingly steep and long that there used to be a funicular railway there. Dylan promptly accepted the challenge; his brakes failed, and a gristle-fracture left him with his famous bulbous and pliable nose. I don't think that men of his own stature offered him any temptation to violence, but large men, or a number of men, offered a challenge. Sometimes Dylan would return from a short visit to London looking like a tomcat after a particularly active night. Perhaps it is an oversimplification to say that large men tend to be peaceable, but I think there is some truth in it. I remember the facial expressions — expressions of blank disbelief — of some large men who met Dylan for the first time, when the scene suddenly changed from one of cordiality and good humour to one of rage and, perhaps, violence; to them it must have been like finding a cobra in a jar of honey.

One evening I conducted a piece of mine at the Royal Albert Hall. It was a double occasion: the first time I conducted at a Prom, and the first performance of the piece. Dylan and I went to the Gargoyle to celebrate, and our loud Welsh voices were easily overheard by a large man at the next table, who began to talk to me about the music, asking what seemed to be quite reasonable questions. I answered willingly, and all was peace. Suddenly Dylan leapt to his feet, his face deep red, his eyes popping, and bellowed: 'Nobody patronizes a friend of *mine*.' The large man's face paled, and a glazed look came into his eyes. Without looking away, he placed on the table a large banknote, taken at random from his pocket, and quickly left the club. Whether the stranger had been sarcastic or not I don't know; if he had been, in my innocence or insensitivity I had not suspected it. But Dylan felt *himself* insulted — incidentally through me. The exact phraseology of his protest is significant.

Sometimes Dylan's outbursts were more amusing than shocking. At one party when I was having a friendly chat with a Very Important B.B.C. Personage, he elbowed his way through the crowd to us and suddenly said to the V.I.B.B.C.P. in a voice that carried through the room: 'If you took off your spectacles and sat on the fire, the room would be full of the smell of roast pork.'

Dylan, in short, welcomed hostile confrontations with strong or influential people. On the other hand, if he was rude it was by intention, never by accident. Here Dylan differed from me very markedly. I was quite outstanding in the number and enormity of my gaffes. 'Dan,' he said to me one day, 'your tact has improved; it is now that of a buffalo.'

Dylan's moral courage was as strong as that of all but the most exceptional people; that is, it was weak, and nothing much can be said about it. His attitude to death was perhaps more remarkable. The reader is free to reject my view that religion, in the ordinary sense of the word, was irrelevant here to his attitude. He was strongly attracted by the poetry of belief and repelled by the absence of poetry in unbelief, but this did not make him a 'believer'. Dylan feared death and at the same time constantly lived under its spell. Death attracted and repelled him equally. He wanted to die soon in some sense that would not actually involve dying, and he hoped to live eternally. While this conflict went on, he was very conscious of the passage of time, bringing him nearer to the end or to another beginning, and he marked that passage in poems. To say that the love and the fear of death co-exist in most men is perhaps a commonplace; what was not common in Dylan was his ability to give expression to this contradiction in his work.

Dylan may or may not have had confidants with whom he discussed his relations with women; I was certainly not one of them. Some tacit understanding, some feeling of delicacy I can't explain made the subject almost taboo between us. I can recall only one exception, and that was more in the nature of a game or a joke than a serious confidence. On Dylan's return from one of his visits to the United States, he gave me an anthology of contemporary American verse which contained, as an appendix, a very large collection of photographs of poets:

I deliberately avoid naming the book. Pointing to some of the women poets, Dylan began chanting, 'Slept with her. Slept with her. Slept with her' and so on. Keeping up the game with its cretic rhythm, I pointed ironically to one of the homelier-looking lady poets and asked, 'Slept with her?' Dylan answered: 'Could have done. Brushed her off.' But this was a game, not to be taken seriously.

On the subject of Dylan's relations with women, I am a poor informant, relying on a little deduction and much guesswork. His dress and manners scarcely classified him as of the genus Casanova. This may have been misleading, but if he paid to women any of those subtle assiduous attentions to which they are reputed to respond, he must have done so in strict privacy. His steady drinking created few opportunities for calculated seduction, still fewer for consummation, and beer, his main drink, is a soporific, not an aphrodisiac.

Frustration, not fulfilment, may be the key to the obsession with sex that permeates Dylan's work. I have in mind not only the poems written in adolescence, between 1930 and 1934, when the obsession would be natural, but all his work, to the very end. *Under Milk Wood*, for example, is a substantial piece, written by a distinguished author in his late thirties, and containing some of his best poetry (the Rosie Probert – Captain Cat sequences); yet it is full of school-boy sex jokes. Perhaps I am at fault here. It could be argued that this is good 'theatre'; certainly, these passages draw the greatest response from the audience, if we rule out the few listeners who are not laughing, but writhing. Shaw, too, knew how to tickle the audience with embarrassingly obvious passages, and even Shakespeare by similar devices sometimes descended to groundling level.

Dylan didn't like to be alone. He once said to me, 'I don't like to wake up alone in the morning.' But perhaps the real presence was never as good as the imagined ideal, and the ideal could not remain intact unless, as with Mog Edwards and Myfanwy Price, it was kept at a distance. If this is a true

51

account of the state of affairs, the situation must have become more and more embarrassing as Dylan became more famous. A novelist said cynically — not these exact words, but words to this effect: 'These cultured literary women will speak to you for ages about your writing, but only with a small part of their minds; the greater part will be concentrated on wondering how soon they can decently jump into bed with you.' Dylan knew this routine; he knew that it required of him to make at least some half-hearted token advances. Probably, in that lionizing atmosphere, sometimes even his most feeble, automatic compliances with the ritual would score success; but it might be the kind of success that is certainly unwelcome in recall, and perhaps not welcome even at the time.

Much has been written and said about Dylan and his drinking; most of it is misleading. To the teetotaller, no doubt, Dylan would seem a heavy drinker. Judgment about this must be comparative. Most of my friends and acquaintances drank every day a fair amount of alcohol, especially in the form of beer, graduating in the evening perhaps to stronger stuff. By their standards, Dylan was a steady and habitual, not a heavy hardened drinker.

The hardened drinker might be recognized by the fact that no amount of alcohol could affect his behaviour, that is, his speech, walk, actions or manner; in fact, I held the theory that in such a case no one could meet the original personality, since its place had been entirely usurped by a new, alcoholic — often rather inscrutable personality.

The heavy drinker was simply fond of more, more and more drink. He it was who devised cunning schemes to bridge the gap between licensing hours with afternoon or all-night clubs, Turkish baths, Thames river trips, and so on. It is surprising how many of my circle claimed at seven in the morning to have become overnight bona fide Covent Garden porters. The Thames river trip, devised to occupy the awkward Sunday afternoon gap, was the brilliant inspiration of my friend the novelist P.L., who had the distinction of causing the boat — after its departure — to turn back to the Westminster jetty to throw him off as a reward for his loud witty commentary on the guide's commentary. These heavy drinkers *were* affected by alcohol, passing in the course of twenty-four hours through two or three crises, marked by unsteadiness, incoherence, euphoria, vomiting, and sleep, from which they recovered to begin the cycle again, taking their second or third 'wind'. It was possible to know and like these men, and, apart from the intervals of insensibility, to take pleasure in their company. You could become fond of them as friends, because you encountered their true characters which, far from being inscrutable, were often more clearly revealed by alcohol.

Dylan cannot be fitted neatly into either of these two categories. For example, night regularly found Dylan well tucked up in bed, his cherubic face innocently snug on the pillow, where he would sleep without interruption till morning. It is true that his day was a succession of pints of beer, but the first four of these slurred his speech, and each pint after that brought him nearer to sleep. Unlike 'hardened' cases, he was exclusively a social drinker. When travelling on the 'Guiness Express', as we called the morning Oxford to London train, Dylan and I used to drink about seven Guinesses each before arrival; he told me that he used to drink only one or two when making the journey alone. Again, unlike most 'heavy' cases, once Dylan sank into sleep, it was unusual for him to rouse himself and take a 'second wind'; sleep, whether on the floor or in bed, lasted till morning.

What I have just written has probably given rise to perplexity in the reader's mind about the causes of Dylan's death. That was my intention. There are some facts, however, that are incontrovertible. I communicated over the Atlantic with the doctor in charge of Dylan's case at St Vincent's and he confirmed that treatment was being directed to an alcoholic coma. Death, presumably from this cause, occurred on 9 November 1953.

Dylan's collapse, however, occurred five days before this, and there is mystery in the circumstances of the collapse. It has been stated that Dylan, *unable to sleep*, got up, and, with company readily available, went *by himself* to drink the fatal amount of whisky. All this is most unusual, but, of course, I cannot say that it is impossible. By all accounts, some of them very lengthy and circumstantial, 'everyone was somewhere else' at the crucial time. The direct cause of his death is known; the primary cause of his death will, it seems, always remain a mystery.

6

Culture, and so forth

'Literature.' Dylan had a special way of uttering this word. He didn't spit it out or say it with a snarl. It was as if he had suddenly bitten into a sloe or a stick of green rhubarb. His mouth screwed away to the left, and the cigarette that always dangled there quivered and drooped dejectedly. A slave uttering the name of a hard task-master? No; it was more like the revulsion many of us feel when people speak of 'your good self' or 'your lady wife'. The word 'literature' meant for Dylan the dead body of something he loved, something killed and embalmed by academics and desecrated by scholarly dissertation.

But literature can wait for a while; in the meantime, there are other subjects that claim consideration.

It is surprising, and perhaps will be incredible to the reader, how many of these other subjects turn out to be irrelevant. The light of Dylan's interest and attention was narrowly focused on a single area, and everything around this was shrouded in darkness. All systematic studies based on observation, calculation or conjecture were abandoned to this outer darkness, that is, to use simpler and more general terms, all subjects with names ending in -ology, -onomy, -ography, -osophy, -ic, -ics, or even, to a large extent, just -y (history, botany).

But this is an exaggeration, to be corrected at once. The area on which the light was focused did not consist entirely of the art of the written or spoken word; there was also to be found there a deep understanding of the motives, feelings and conduct of human beings, though psychology, in the strict sense of the word, was excluded as a member of the '-ology' species. Again, the light-dark metaphor holds good only if it is understood that, instead of a sharp dividing line, there was a shading-off. Nearest to the light came the 'other arts'; Dylan was conscious of them even if he did not appreciate their possibilities. Then, in a sort of penumbra, I would place his awareness of visible 'nature'.

Since this may shock the romantic reader, I shall break the news gently. I am not saying that Dylan couldn't see any difference between a sunflower and a violet, a buzzard and a goldfinch, a butterfly and an earthworm, I am only suggesting that this recognition, instead of being instantaneous, as it is with most of us, required from him a split second's thought; in other words, his unconscious power of attention to 'observable nature' was, I think, below the average.

On the other hand, if observation was directly relevant to his central interests, and only in that case, he could observe, and where the relevance was great, his observation could be keen. To take 'buzzard' as an example. If no purpose was to be served, Dylan could ignore both the bird and the word. But if it suited his purpose, he could take possession of both, and present the complete entity of 'buzzard', its buzzardry, in a way that is, of course, very rare.*

I am uncomfortably aware that Dylan's dismissal of '-ologies', as I have described it, may have offended some to whom such things are dear; my excuse is the disinterested search for truth in the particular task I have set myself. Not all books and essays on Dylan Thomas have been written purely with this aim; many writers, consciously or unconsciously, have liked nothing better than to give free wing to the bees in their bonnets, to mould the truth to the form of their desires, and even, oh, horror! to display their 'erudition'. No, Dylan

---

* My subject here is limited to Dylan's powers of observation as they are related to his poetry; I do not want to give the impression that he was at all vague or absent-minded in practical matters. In the business of day-to-day living, unlike Vernon Watkins, he knew a 'hawk from a handsaw'.

Thomas did not know by heart the Koran, the Zend Avesta, the Upanishads, the Lun Yü, and had no access to the Kabbala. He knew well all the finest literary passages of the Bible (the 1611 Version, of course) for purely literary reasons, but would have failed the most elementary Sunday School test on biblical 'knowledge'. To him, Jericho might just as well have been a person as a place; but the addition of the Jericho ingredient to a poem, like the 'Jack Christ' ingredient, could, he knew, induce a religious impression, in the same way as a mustard sandwich without ham can be imagined to be a ham sandwich with mustard.

Among the '-ologies' there are some '-ics', and of these it is perhaps necessary to mention only politics. Politics never played any significant part in Dylan's life or work. In his youth, he came under the influence of a much older man, Bert Trick, who pressed upon him writings of Marx and Lenin, which Dylan did not understand and could not read; Dylan tried to pass these ideas on to me, but in such a garbled form that I couldn't understand them either. I suppose that at this period he might have been called a tepid communist. At the time of the Spanish Civil War there were many artists a good deal angrier with Hitler and Mussolini when they attacked distant Spain than they became later on when those gentlemen attacked the homeland. Dylan was seen much in the company of these artists and was their friend, but it would be a mistake to assume that he shared their views in any but the most superficial way. These two historical events did not deeply affect him or his writings. But I must emphasize that I say this only with politics in mind. In the humanitarian sense, everything was very different. The senseless killing, mutilation, torture, starvation and loss of liberty profoundly moved him, all political considerations set aside.

Dylan had small knowledge and appreciation of the visual arts, and no skill in them. But it is not at all irrelevant to discuss this. First of all, such a bald statement must be given supporting evidence. Though he lived a long time in London, and visited

Italy and the U.S.A., he made no effort to frequent galleries, and the visual arts did not enter into his conversation, his lectures or, with very few exceptions, his writings. He knew few paintings and few painters; I mean by this that he could distinguish only a few painters from one another, and only a few styles of painting from one another. Dylan's preferences were influenced by literary considerations; where these were absent or very marginal in a painting, he showed little interest, but where they were of some importance, as may happen to be the case in some great works, he expressed approval. To give one example: Dylan liked Hieronymus Bosch, not because of the fine painting of this master, but because of the literary aspect of his images, which fascinated him.

In 1936, a notable exhibition of surrealist work was held at New Burlington Galleries in London, and one afternoon Dylan and I visited it together. It was great fun. There was a complete tea-set made of squirrel's fur, the fur, of course, on the *inside*. There was a conventional landscape which attracted us both in different ways; Dylan liked the huge safety-pin painted right across the sky, while I admired the grass, which had precisely the same quality and texture as the fur on a Landseer animal. A huge picture of a nude woman strikingly emphasized the bilateral design of the human body by restricting the left half to the two-dimensional, while the right half was allowed to blossom into three dimensions; from the projecting nipple there hung a thin chain, on this there swung a cage, and in the cage there fidgeted and cleaned its whiskers a white mouse. As I looked at it, I felt a pair of eyes boring through the back of my skull. Turning, I saw the room attendant, glaring ferociously, but not at me. I went up to him for a cosy chat, thinking to cheer him up a little. His grievance burst out from him at once. 'I'm supposed to keep that bloody mouse watered and fed. As Exhibition Attendant, it isn't part of my Recognized Duties. Man and boy I've been et cetera et cetera, in all my born days et cetera', and he subsided, muttering darkly something about

unions.* There were some exhibits that would now be called
'mobiles', but in those days they didn't move. Dylan and I
modified several of these with deft tweaks; our activities went
undetected then, and perhaps even afterwards, but in any case
what we did was in strict accordance with the prevailing
atmosphere of the exhibition. It was fun, good *literary* fun.

Dylan wisely restricted his own efforts to squiggly lines, and
in this doodling he sometimes created a certain serendipity.
Influenced by Thurber, or perhaps deliberately following the
procedure Thurber himself admits, Dylan often added some
really funny captions. Here are two examples:

> (Beneath two heads, facing one another):
>
> He: I've swallowed my toothbrush, by Jove!
> She: So you have, you foolish Lothario.
>
> (One recognizable figure, looking round, followed by a figure
> unrecognizable):
>
> There's something abstract following me.

However, for a few sentences at least, Dylan did once become
an Art Critic. He was staying with me at the time, and had
Naomi Mitchison's *Beyond this Limit* to review. He gave the
book a terrible slating. He laid down his pencil, thinking that he
had completed the review, but then remembered that he had
not mentioned the illustrations, which were by Wyndham
Lewis, and, taking it up again, added in the margin: 'The
drawings remind me of Picasso under the influence of Thurber,
but not so funny. Every one of them is ugly, pointless,
meaningless, careless, affected. Some of them remind me of
those designs on toilet paper that are not always done by hand.'

* I would like to forestall the criticism of any reader who may have visited the
same exhibition and found in the cage not a live mouse but a stuffed one, or,
indeed, no mouse at all. I commiserate with him. The creature had to be
exercised. Wearing a diamanté collarette, it was led around the gallery once a day
on a leash. This piquant spectacle merited a place in the Catalogue, number 451b,
if my memory does not fail me, not for sale, and called 'La Promenade de la
Souris'.

My Friend Dylan Thomas

To me, not to some perhaps, but to me, Dylan's poetry is not visual; it does not evoke spontaneous visual images in my mind. I must make clear that the distinction I myself make between descriptive poetry and visual poetry is this: in descriptive poetry we are told what things would look like if we could see them, while in visual poetry we are made to see those things as images in the mind. This distinction, of course, is a personal one, and since it may not be shared, I give here some examples of verse I consider 'visual'.

From Dante:

> Io vidi due ghiacciati in una buca
> sì che l'un capo all'altro era cappello.

(*Inferno xxxii*)

(I saw two frozen in a hole so that one head served as a hat to the other.)

From Chaucer:

> And with that water that ran so cleer
> My face I wissh. Tho saugh I wel
> The botme paved everydel
> With gravel, ful of stones shene.

(*The Romaunt of the Rose*)

From Eliot:

> And now a gusty shower wraps
> The grimy scraps
> Of withered leaves about your feet
> And newspapers from vacant lots;
> The showers beat
> On broken blinds and chimney-pots,
> And at the corner of the street
> A lonely cab-horse steams and stamps.
> And then the lighting of the lamps.

(*Preludes I*)

In that very visually conscious century, the eighteenth, poetry of this kind is common, and sometimes the poet straight-

60

forwardly invites the reader to use his inner eye: 'View now the winter storm!' (Crabbe: *The Borough*).

I am far from suggesting that visual poetry is necessarily good. I believe that this characteristic, visuality, is as unrelated to the quality of poetry as the power of some music to evoke visual images is to the quality of the music. My contention is that the occurrence of descriptive passages in Dylan's work, and they are very frequent, should not lead us into thinking that in them his aim was to evoke spontaneous visual images. The slowly unfolding complex texture of the words works against this. What a contrast to the simple hard directness of the Dante, Chaucer and Eliot quotations, which are intended to reveal an immediate picture!

Many readers will no doubt contend that the evidence of *Under Milk Wood* alone refutes my point. I shall stick to my guns. The 'prose' of the two narrators, thickly larded with adjectives, single or even multiple, and stretched into catalogues in the manner of Robert Burton or James Joyce, is typical of the descriptive style. It was a brilliant stroke to make blind Captain Cat a third narrator, because, without any expectation of using his eyes, the listener will find natural the substitution of sound for sight in this *Play for Voices*.

It is a relief to leave this subject, on which I have had to put forward some controversial opinions, for another which I can introduce at once with a statement not likely to be disputed. Dylan's ear for the sound of words was exceptional. But wait. Isn't there some snare, some sly condition lurking in the phrase 'for the sound of words'? There is.

A literary man of some eminence, Gilbert Murray, I think, once stated categorically that the poet's ear is finer than the musician's. When I read this, my reactions passed through three stages. First, there was a feeling of indignation, based on personal prejudice. Then, realizing my bias, I turned to reasoning. If the statement was true, the whole subject of music could be mastered *en passant* and left behind by any poet; but this seems never to have happened. I came to my senses only at the third stage: music is not sound, sound is not music, and the comparison itself was illogical.

Nature is full of beautiful sounds, including the sounds of words, with which it would be illogical to compare music as an art-form. This is what I take it that Cocteau means when he writes, 'Le rossignol chante mal'.* Who would expect even the lyre-bird, the nightingale's Australian rival, to play the part of Mozart's Queen of the Night? The great ornithologist, Ludwig Koch, knew a great deal about bird-song, but he was not as good a musician as another Ludwig, who knew comparatively little. Milton's father was a composer, and Milton himself, arguably the most 'musical' of all English poets, was an accomplished musician. This sort of thing is very gratifying to everybody, but it seems to hold true all too seldom for poets after the Jacobean era; on the contrary, however mellifluous their verse, however cunningly they manipulate the sounds of words, in general they seem to remain thoroughly uninterested in music and unaware of its true nature.

Among my artist friends and acquaintances, the painters and the sculptors are the most appreciative of music; perhaps, through aptitude and training, like mathematicians they can accept that something significant may be conveyed by means other than words. This acceptance seems to come with great difficulty to writers.† They are voluble on the subject, of course, as, for example, Baudelaire was, but what they have to say usually only serves to expose their lack of appreciation more quickly to the musician.

Since I have embarked on a digression, I may as well finish it with the description of an incident from my hoard of embarrassing experiences. I was associated in a TV broadcast

* *Le Rappel à l'Ordre* (Paris, 1926, p. 18).
† To say that my opinions here are limited to writers of my acquaintance would be the coward's way; I am prepared to let them stand as applicable to writers in a general sense. The notable exceptions (Henry Carey, E. T. A. Hoffmann, Samuel Butler, Romain Rolland and Thomas Mann, for example) remain exceptions; they have to be searched out.

with an ostentation of writers — have I the correct generic
term? Since this was an occasion of some importance, the
B.B.C. gave us an excellent meal. My colleagues, all strangers to
me, exerted themselves to be courteous, that is to say,
condescending, by confining the conversation to music, since
they assumed that I would be unwilling to try to speak about
anything else; whereas, as the reader will have discovered by
now, this is far from being the case. The display of useless
learning was impressive. One casually mentioned the name of
the first tenor to sing Pinkerton at La Scala; the Köchel number
of Mozart's Andante for Barrel-organ dropped from the lips of
another; while a third rattled off the genealogy of one of
Offenbach's mistresses. I did not know any of these things, and
cared not a hoot for them. But I became more and more
depressed as I recognized what I call 'compensatory knowledge'; in other words, these knowledgeable people were
compensating for the fact that they could not tell one tune
from another.

Dylan has been waiting in the wings during this digression;
now he enters, not alone, but in the company of other writers.
Yes, he too was musically illiterate. There is no harm in that, of
course. Since this book is written, not in German or Czech, but
in English, the likelihood is that ninety per cent of my readers
will also be musically illiterate. This does not bring with it a
lack of appreciation of music, but there are certain disadvan-
tages. It is possible to love literature without learning to read;
but any increase of knowledge and appreciation must then
depend on public readings or theatrical performances. Dylan
did not seek the compensations of the concert-hall, the
opera-house, the record-library, and remained ignorant of
musical works — with one significant exception: *Il Trovatore*!
And about *Il Trovatore* there is a story.

One day, when Dylan met me in a Chelsea pub, I found him
in a state of great excitement. He had been lent an old
gramophone and an album of *Il Trovatore*, speed 78. 'It's
great!' he kept saying, between pints, 'Great!' We took some

flagons back to the Manresa Road studio, and there sat the dirty old machine, with, as I noticed at once, its speed regulator pointing to Maximum. 'What about this speed gadget, Dylan?' I asked, as he got ready to put on a record. 'That thing? It's stuck. Makes no difference.' But it did make a difference, to me at any rate. By some mechanical quirk, the music turned out to be exactly an octave too high, exactly twice the right speed. Love duets were performed by *tenori crudelmente castrati* and *sopranini ottavinetti*; their ecstasy was consummated in double-quick time while the piccolo got lost in regions of pitch audible only to dogs and bats. The *Anvil Chorus* sounded strangely like the frenzied dwarf-hammerings in *Das Rheingold*. Dylan was delighted, particularly with the hectic passion of the tenors. 'Those Italian tenors,' he cried, 'wear their testicles in their throats!' So that was where they had gone.

This incident is oddly connected with another that occurred many years later in a Swansea pub. Dylan was telling me about his first meeting with Stravinsky, which had just taken place in the U.S.A. They got on very well together, and among the reasons for this rapport not least significant was the following exchange. The Maestro: 'What is your favourite music?' Dylan: '*Il Trovatore*!' (The only music he knew, in fact). Anyone who reads what Stravinsky has written about himself, or what John Cage and others have written about Stravinsky, will realize that Dylan could not have made a better impression than he did with that reply.

The occasion for the meeting between Stravinsky and Dylan was the commission of an opera from them both by Boston University. Nothing was decided at this first meeting, but Stravinsky prepared for Dylan's next visit by having an independent annex built on to his house for Dylan's sole use during their collaboration; they never met again.

In the meantime, Dylan spent much time discussing the commission with me. We ourselves had often talked of collaborating in an opera, and were in agreement on several points in the libretto, for example, that, Fidelio-like, it should have as its central theme the winning of freedom from oppression. But this was a different situation. I felt I had to warn Dylan that in Stravinsky he would find someone who would not agree too readily to any suggestions; someone who might turn out to be immovably obstinate in his insistence on his own firmly established ideas. Secretly, in spite of the auspicious personal beginning, I could not imagine a happy collaboration between them that would endure the tests of time, conflict of opinion and contrasting work-habits. I showed Dylan a vocal score of *The Rake's Progress* and he skimmed through the libretto, constantly picking holes in Auden's text. I myself thought Auden's words skilful and clever, and the success of this opera — I mean its success in relation to its aims — was another consideration I added to my secret doubts about the proposed collaboration.*

Opinions differ about the suitability of Dylan's poetry for musical use. In the earliest years of our friendship I set many of his poems for voice and piano, and even one enormously long poem, 'The Idyll of Forgetfulness', for the complete salmagundi of soloists, chorus and orchestra (January 1930). All this was appallingly bad stuff, of course, and I mention it only to make the point that as soon as the densely-packed style characteristic of Dylan's serious work developed, I felt, and still feel that his verse became unsuitable for musical setting. Our plans for an opera were only vague, and if anything at all had come of them, one of my principal difficulties, I secretly felt, would be to persuade Dylan to adopt a simpler and more straightforward style. At the same time, I should perhaps add the words 'by me' to the phrase 'suitable for musical setting'. There is no reason why my opinion should be shared, and to some extent it has not been shared. Many of my contemporaries, including Stravinsky (*In Memoriam*), have felt that they could use, and presumably have been happy to use Dylan's words.

* This is a good illustration of the fact that my book is written strictly from my point of view. To *Stravinsky* Dylan diplomatically praised Auden (see Robert Craft: *Conversations with Stravinsky*).

My Friend Dylan Thomas

At first sight it might seem that the music to *Under Milk Wood*, which I wrote at Dylan's express wish, contradicts all I have said. I am not thinking of this kind of thing. These songs are not in Dylan's serious poetic style any more than they are in my serious musical style. He probably took one morning over the words, just as I took one morning over the music; the collaboration was for a particular, a special purpose.

As the reader can well imagine, Dylan and I seldom talked for any length of time or with any seriousness about music; he couldn't, and I didn't want to. I happen to remember only three exchanges between us:

D.T.   Why is your music so *pure*?
D.J.   It is not pure enough by a very, very long way.

D.T.   Why don't you write like Ravel?
D.J.   Because I don't want to.

D.T.   I like the 'unexpected note'.
D.J.   You can get the 'unexpected note' only after you've written enough 'expected notes'.

It would be natural to suppose that no one could practice the art of combining words in verse-patterns without realizing a connection between his art and musical influences. So the Greek chorus danced in the orchestra with precision to the sounds of the appropriate modes and, turning from right to left in the strophe, and from left to right in the antistrophe, carefully adjusted their movements in accordance with the poetic feet. But spondees, iambs, trochees, anapaests, dactyls, amphibrachs, amphimacers, could have been so many primeval monsters to Dylan, and their ancient heavy tread had indeed as little relevance to his verse. To him, prosody was one of the obnoxious '-y' subjects.* Early in his development as a writer,

---

* In this book, as the reader has already been warned, I am purposely avoiding any direct reference to Dylan's serious work, but from time to time I cannot help skirting the subject. I have written a long note on Dylan's verse-patterns in *Dylan Thomas: The Poems* (Dent, 1971, pp. 245-9).

Dylan passed through and left behind two stages in the technique of versification: the normal accentual system, and the system, then much in vogue, of cadenced (so-called 'free') verse. Perhaps on the model of Blake's Prophetic Books, he found what he wanted in the syllabic count, that is, a scheme based on the number of syllables in a line, without regard to the number or the position of stresses. This happened at least as early as the poem 'I dreamed my genesis', written shortly after his twentieth birthday (December 1934).* Dylan could, and did return to accentual metre, for parody, satire, or occasional verse. The strange fact is that even before his final adoption of the 'syllabic count' he acquired the habit of counting syllables on his fingers while composing poetry, and kept this habit throughout his life. He never established in his mind the obvious connection between word-stress and musical accent.

This statement is hard to believe, but here is a story to support it. *John O'London's Weekly* advertised a competition for the best poem that could be sung to the *Londonderry Air*, prize one guinea, and Dylan and I decided to go in for it, writing alternate lines, as usual. 'Do you know the tune?' he asked. I said that I did. 'How many syllables?' 'Twelve ten twelve ten.' 'Right. Let's start!' After I had written my line, I handed the page over, and Dylan set to work, with much finger-counting. When I saw his line, a thousand times better than mine, I was aghast. There were ten syllables all right, but only three stresses. 'Look here, you can't sing the tune to that.' 'Why not? It has ten syllables, hasn't it?' 'Yes, but . . .' But there is no need to continue with the story. It was impossible to explain to Dylan why it does not follow that a phrase of music requiring ten syllables can be sung to *any* ten-syllable line. The paper was torn up in anger. We didn't go in for the competition; probably we wouldn't have won, anyway.

* In the *Note on Verse-Patterns*, already mentioned, I try to express my own personal feeling that this system is not merely artificial, and, as a second line of defence against criticism, I take the view that an artist must accept some form of discipline either from outside or within himself, before he can work at all.

67

Dylan's reading was intensive, rather than extensive. This bald statement cannot be left to stand on its own; perhaps, as it stands, it is not even quite correct. At any rate, I must add a great deal of explanation, and probably some modification.

Dylan's knowledge of languages other than English can at least be dealt with summarily; he had no knowledge of this kind whatsoever. His interest in words was first limited to English words, and then further limited to the way in which they were potentially of use to himself. At the risk of irritating the reader, I must use almost the same phraseology to extend its application to literature: in literature his interest was small or great in proportion to the absence or the presence of certain elements, including words, that could be of use to him.

At the beginning of this chapter I described Dylan's reaction to the word 'literature', and I have stressed more than once his dislike of an academic approach to any subject. I have read somewhere the account of a conference held at an American university; Dylan, the English professor, and a senior class of English students took part. At one point, the professor addressed a complicated, rather long-winded, but penetrating question to Dylan. Dylan 'answered', evidently turning to the students: 'What it is to be *educated*!' The poor professor, publicly crushed, murmured: 'I shall say no more.' And indeed, for the rest of the conference, he said no more.

To understand this cruel story, it is necessary to realize what Dylan meant by 'educated'. To him, education was enforcement to do hard labour, at the best for some very distant reward, or at worst for no reward at all. He would not struggle with French to read Verlaine, with Italian to read Leopardi, with Russian to read Blok, or, to come nearer home, with Old English to read *Beowulf* or with Middle English to read *The Pearl*. Dante, Chaucer, Molière, Goethe, Pushkin, were mere names to him, and, even if he was secretly dissatisfied with this situation, he still was unwilling that it should be otherwise at any cost to himself.

The extent of Dylan's knowledge of literature in the English

68

1. At the Pelican, on the day of the funeral, November 1953
Back row: (from left) Jim Jones, John Ormond, John Prichard, Fred Janes, Irene Jones
Front row: Margaret Taylor, Martha the Death, Charles Fisher, Mably Owen, Daniel Jones, Florence Thomas, Mary Janes
(Photograph by John Chillingworth, *Picture Post*)

language, beginning with Skelton, was uneven, but very concentrated in the areas that interested him. Donne, Sir Thomas Browne, Webster, Traherne, Herbert, Blake — the list can be deduced by the reader from Dylan's own work — were greatly loved, and when Dylan loved a writer, he loved him fervently. He had little sympathy with eighteenth-century literature *in general*, but was fascinated by the group of great eccentrics, for example Swift and Smart, for whom the century is remarkable. His knowledge of nineteenth-century poetry was wide, and it became still more extensive in the course of his radio and public readings. But no one, perhaps, could equal him in his knowledge of twentieth-century literature. It seemed to me that every periodical specializing in contemporary verse, and every new volume of poems, published on both sides of the Atlantic, passed at some time through his hands.*

In spite of the orderly way in which I have tried to describe Dylan's reading, it must not be concluded that his reading was systematic. There was no system, and a great deal of Dylan's reading was accidental. Some of it, like Coleridge's reading of the chronicles of voyages, aroused sudden enthusiasms and affected his work. His ignorance of foreign languages was to a small extent balanced by the fact that translations of certain masterpieces, for example, of Rabelais, Ibsen and Lorca, to name three extremely different writers, sometimes fell into his hands. When a book was too massive to be absorbed in its entirety, Burton's *The Anatomy of Melancholy*, Frazer's *The Golden Bough*, or Doughty's *Arabia Deserta*, perhaps, Dylan dipped into it and found treasures, as well as sources for his

---

* These words might be misunderstood, especially by anyone who has read my note to Poem 79 in *Dylan Thomas: The Poems* (1971, p. 258). In that note I describe the alacrity with which, as an unknown poet, he joined the Victor Neuberg circle, in spite of the fact that I, in my rather priggish way, had ridiculed it. Dylan's interest in his contemporaries was very genuine; he wanted to know what they were writing and, when praise was deserved, he expressed it freely. He also wanted to find out what periodical editors liked, how strong the 'competition' was, and how to promote his own work; but all this was subsidiary to his genuine interest.

69

2.   At the old B.B.C. Studio, The Grove, Swansea, October 1949
Standing: John Griffiths (B.B.C. producer)
Seated: (from left) Vernon Watkins, John Prichard, Fred Janes, Daniel Jones, Dylan Thomas
(*South Wales Evening Post* photograph)

own work. *Ulysses* and *Finnegan's Wake*, on the other hand, were consumed whole, and ruminated upon.

By implying influences, I am coming dangerously close to a subject I undertook to avoid: direct comment upon Dylan's work. In spite of this, I cannot resist giving two more examples. While Dylan was sketching the first drafts of *UnderMilk Wood*, he showed great enthusiasm for *The Oxford Dictionary of Nursery Rhymes* (1951) and read me some extracts; the connection with the children's songs in the play is obvious.* Finally, there is Gerard Manley Hopkins. Any suggestion that he was influenced by Hopkins threw Dylan into a rage: a significant reaction. It was this suggestion, even more than the chapter entitled 'Is Dylan a Fake?', that infuriated Dylan when he read Henry Treece's *Dylan Thomas* (1949). Alluding to a popular song of the time, he said to me bitterly, 'Only God could make a Treece'. The offending chapter, 'The Debt to Hopkins', ends with a parallel list of compound words used by Hopkins and by Dylan, for example 'manshape', 'Jackself', 'Jackchrist', that clinches the argument, if indeed there really is any argument.†

Like all writers, Dylan worked with a few reference books within reach. Apart from ordinary dictionaries, there were Walker's Rhyming Dictionary and Roget's Thesaurus. I was surprised, I must admit, to find that Dylan used Roget when writing poetry, and I didn't know about this until after his death, when I happened to see some figures scrawled in the margin of a recently composed poem; at first I couldn't understand them, but then it occurred to me that they were Roget numbers. They were, and the discovery made me modify

---

* I remember Dylan's delighted statement that the Swansea area is the richest in the country for children's songs and game-songs; this seems to be supported by Iona and Peter Opie in their book, *The Lore and Language of School-children* (O.U.P. 1959). The Index of the book gives eighty-four references to Swansea, and half that number, for example, to Edinburgh.

† An account of the Treece-Thomas relationship will be found in my note to Poem 117 in *Dylan Thomas: The Poems* (Dent, 1971, p. 267).

to some extent the opinion I was inclined to hold about the relative importance Dylan gave to word-meaning.

In pointing out the limitations of Dylan's reading, I have no derogatory intention. He could do without certain things, so why not do without them? Breadth of reading is no doubt splendid in itself, but it is certainly not a necessary condition of literary 'genius'. The stages of Keats's reading can be marked in his work, Milton, Homer, Dante, Dryden; on the other hand, this does not imply that he would have been a better poet if he had possessed Matthew Arnold's breadth of knowledge. The magnificence of Milton's poetry sometimes actually seems to be achieved *in spite of* vast erudition. Shakespeare was well served by North, Holinshed and Ovid. Not every poet can, or need be a polymath like Goethe, or have the intellectual scope and discipline of Dante. Burns, forgive me, Scottish readers, had no unusually extensive knowledge of literature, and named as his favourite book, next to the Bible, the 'novel of sentiment' Henry MacKenzie's *Man of Feeling*.* All this is even more forcibly true of John Clare and William Barnes, for example. In all the range of poets, from so-called 'greatest' to so-called 'less great', one thing seems to remain true: like animals feeding on what they physically need, berries, insects, fish, other animals, they waste no time on the superfluous; in other words, they conform with the economy of animals, which is based on the rule that there shall be no waste of food, effort or activity. The wren has no more taste for rabbit than the eagle has for grass-seeds.

It is hardly likely that anyone with enough interest in Dylan Thomas to be reading these words is not already familar, through tapes, discs or broadcasts, with the rich sonority of his voice and the impressiveness of his verse interpretations. Any direct treatment of this subject would probably seem an impertinence, but some comment here would not be out of place.

* Letter to John Murdoch, 15 January 1783.

My Friend Dylan Thomas

First of all, there is a possible misunderstanding to be cleared up. Dylan, like his father, had no discernible Welsh accent; or, if he had one, it was scarcely discernible. Any misunderstanding about this must be laid to the door of certain actors, Welsh and non-Welsh, and would-be imitators of Dylan. Here I may be guilty of personal prejudice, because it is particularly to a Welsh ear that a sham Welsh accent is so offensive. There seem to be two motives for this public misrepresentation of Dylan: personal vanity, and a false idea of the performer's task. Vanity whispers: 'As a professional, I can "do" an Irish accent, a Lancashire accent, et cetera, and I'm not going to let *them* think that I can't "do" a Welsh accent.' Duty prompts: 'As a professional, my task is to "put Dylan across", and this means I must assume my Welsh accent.' These people serve up to the public the falsehood it expects rather than the truth it deserves; let me assure them that being a Welshman is a full-time job.

I may seem inconsistent later on, when I stress, as I must, the Welshness of Dylan's reading. In the meantime, I merely point out that there is a great difference between a Welsh accent on the one hand, and a Welsh intonation and style of speaking on the other.

It may be trite to say this, but it must be said: just because someone has written a poem, it does not follow that he is able to read it aloud to others. The vogue, if I may call it that, for the public reading of poems by their authors has more of a financial basis than an artistic one. Pity the poor poet. His fee on the platform may be more than all the earnings from his slim volume, and there may well be more people in the audience to hear him than there are to buy it. Therefore, let him have his recital. Unfortunately, these occasions are often embarrassing. The listeners may be embarrassed because the poet, with whom they sympathize to a painful degree, manifestly cannot read his poem; or the poet is himself embarrassed by his situation and communicates his embarrassment to the audience. The alternative, the only important one, gives rise to a distinct style of reading, withdrawn and detached. It is as if the poet were saying: 'Outside the hall I saw a piece of paper in the gutter. I picked it up and found that it contained words all cut up into lines; a poem, perhaps? Anyway, I'm going to read this to myself, however much it bores me to do so, and if you happen to eavesdrop, I suppose I can't stop you.'

The consistent failure of such efforts in public leads to one conclusion only: for these occasions the poet *must* un-ashamedly put on a performance. In an earlier chapter I mentioned that Dylan pitched his professional voice for the reading of serious verse about a major sixth below his natural voice. At the time, the reader may have thought that my remark indicated sardonic disapproval. On the contrary, I think that the adoption of this device, and of similar 'artificial' devices, was well justified. For Dylan, the reading of serious poetry aloud was a special activity; for this he refused to use the same voice with which he might ask, 'When's the next train to Carmarthen?'

I have stressed the word 'serious' in the last paragraph, because Dylan had at least three distinct reading styles, and to one of these, reserved for non-serious texts, all that is true of the others in pitch and tempo does not apply. For humorous scripts Dylan normally used his tenor voice and spoke fast; only too often he sounds breathless and over-excited, as if he had just run up and down a flight of stairs several times, or as if someone were tickling the soles of his feet as he read. In fairness, it should be added that sometimes he was probably performing under time pressure, with a twenty-minute script to compress into fifteen minutes.

The readings for which Dylan is justly admired are his readings of serious poetry in a baritone or bass-baritone voice when, of course, he was 'on form', not drunk, and guarded by the microphone from the heady influence of a living audience. These fortunately have been captured for all time on tape and record.

The tempo of such readings as these is uniformly slow. The slowness pleased me very much; gabbled Shakespeare, for

example, had always been one of my pet dislikes.* At Dylan's
speed, full value was given to every vowel, every consonant.
One day I teased him about this slowness, though I admired it,
and said so. With stop-watch in hand, I invited him to read the
first line of Blake's *The Book of Thel*:

> The daughters of the Seraphim led round their sunny flocks.

The whole line took twelve seconds! I was particularly struck
by his pronunciation 'F-L-O-C-K-S', which lasted three
seconds; he pronounced it 'ffloc-kss', the 'c' and the 'k' quite
separate: it was impossible to confuse it with 'phlox'. Allowing
one-and-a-half seconds between lines, I worked out that it
would take twenty-five minutes to read the whole poem, not
counting Thel's Motto. Of course, Dylan could see the
stop-watch in my hand, and probably exaggerated his slowness
for my benefit, but the experiment was still significant.

My choice of *The Book of Thel* was no accident; readers who
remember my earlier remarks about Dylan's system of versification will appreciate my reasons. Here, as in his readings of
his own poetry, there was not only very little change in tempo,
but unusually little ictus or rhythmical forward motion. This
kind of reading was very suitable for Dylan's syllable-counting
system of versification. The listener, distracted as little as
possible by stress or pulsation, was actually able to feel, for
example, that in the course of a verse he had travelled through
thirteen or fourteen full syllabic units. A complete poem read
in this way had a cumulative effect that was incantatory,
almost hypnotic. At the same time, by this means the timbre of
consonants and vowels drew the attention away from the literal
sense to the allusive implication of words.

Dylan's third style of reading was not his best, and he was
well aware of the fact. Discussing this with me, he confessed in
despondent tones, 'I'm just a failed ham Charles Laughton.'
The transition to the third style was the result not so much of

---

* I would offer, as a test, the words 'Othello's occupation's gone,' the difference
between triviality and greatness depending on the tempo.

drink as of the presence of an audience. All had paid to see and hear him, to admire, to be entertained, or even shocked. He served up what was expected of him. With eyes starting out of a purple face, neck swelling, clothes appropriately disordered, Dylan would bellow and boom like a big man locked in a cupboard. His voice took on the fruitiness of wines made from vineyards growing too far south. The timbre sank from the bronchial to the borborygmic, and sometimes even to the prorumpt.* Those who came to be entertained had their money's worth: the exhibition of a poet, a Welshman, none too sober, uninhibited, everything they securely congratulated themselves on not being, and at the same time with a delicious thrill half-envied.

It is not with this part of Dylan's audience that I am concerned. I am concerned with those of his listeners genuinely moved by his readings. Everyone who has had any experience of a relationship with an audience, a teacher, a musician, an actor, an orator, knows that communication works (or should work) in both directions. The history of Welsh non-conformist preaching provides some of the most striking examples. At the end of the eighteenth and the beginning of the nineteenth centuries enormous congregations met in the fields, listening to and collaborating in sermons lasting for hours. When the chapels were built, the same tradition lived on. The Welsh preachers cultivated a rhetorical device called 'hwyl'; this was in effect a very slow, prolonged crescendo of emotion through all the degrees from quiet detachment and flatness to passionate involvement and fervour.† The occasion was seldom a purely solo performance; as the excitement grew, the con-

---

* This pretty word, which explains itself, is among the spewings of Crispinus in Jonson's *The Poetaster*.

† The word 'hwyl', as it is commonly used, for example to describe the choral transports of a Welsh rugby crowd, is probably untranslatable, but the dictionary meanings are suggestive. One of the meanings is a ship's sail; 'llong hwyliog' is a ship under sail. As the ship lies becalmed at the beginning of its voyage, the sail flaps idly against the mast (hwylbren); the breeze picks up, the sails fill, the wind grows in strength, and the ship flies across the water with ever increasing speed.

gregation usually joined in with cries of 'Haleliwia! Amen!' and 'Felly y bo! Diolch i Dduw! Diolch iddo Ef!'* Dylan's great-uncle, the Rev. William Thomas, was famous in Wales for his sermons, as well as for his poetry, and it is not too far-fetched to assume that this style of oratory was in Dylan's blood.†

The popularity of Dylan's recitals is a reminder of the earlier popularity of Dickens's famous 'monopolyogues'. The extraordinary parallels between Dylan and Dickens (whom Dylan fervently loved) seem never to have been stressed, or perhaps even suggested. Both travelled extensively to give solo public readings of their own works; both earned large sums of money by this means, especially in America; both tried to make their performances impressive, Dylan by 'hwyl', Dickens by extravagant gestures and grimaces;‡ both became so exhausted by this activity that they began to subsist less on food than on drink; to both death came in the end far earlier than one would hope, and as the indirect result of anxiety and fatigue.

Dylan began his broadcasting career rather badly. A B.B.C. friend arranged the engagement for him with some difficulty, because Dylan was not very well known at the time. An hour before the broadcast (live, not recorded) he was in London, not in Cardiff, where he should have been, and then the Soho pubs had to be searched for him: no small task. The programme was to consist of readings of his own verse, but when at last his voice came on the land-line to Cardiff, he began in a thick voice, 'Here are some poems I have liked.' Many a fine performer has survived catastrophe as great as this at his Wigmore Hall début,

---

* 'So be it! Thanks be to God! Thanks be to Him!'

† William Thomas was born on 7 April 1834, in Llandysul, on the river Marles, and died on 11 December 1879. He took as his pen-name Gwilym Marles, after the river beside which he was born, and a collection of his poems, sermons and essays was published in 1905. Dylan's middle name, Marlais, derives from Marles. (See my note to Poem 82 in *Dylan Thomas: The Poems*, 1971).

‡ See *Charles Dickens: The Public Readings*, edited by Philip Collins (O.U.P., 1975).

and Dylan survived, of course, to become one of the finest and most famous of broadcasters. His humorous or nostalgic scripts, perhaps, were the most popular; they have been available on the printed page for a long time now.*

Aneirin Talfan Davies, then head of the Swansea Studios of the B.B.C., was a very good friend to Dylan on many of these occasions. Dylan was always in financial difficulties, and Aneirin, instead of lending him money, wisely gave him work. Since Dylan almost always stayed with me, I was often present at the studio when he recorded. He probably made scores and scores of tapes, but of course only some of these were good enough for broadcasting. Aneirin acted like an older brother on these occasions. Detecting the signs of drink, smoking, or simple fatigue, he would say, 'You're over the edge now, Dylan; let's chuck it.' And we would all go across to The King's Arms for refreshment.

I myself took part with Dylan in only two or three broadcasts. I wrote the script of one of these, which tested Dylan's reading technique to the full; his virtuosity was like that of a pianist who, as musicians say, can 'cover the keyboard' brilliantly and manage the most difficult passages with apparent ease.

In my undergraduate days, I had 'discovered' among the Arber Reprints the so-called translation of Virgil by Richard Stanyhurst, alchemist, renegade priest, and spy in the pay of Philip II. Many years later, when I was going through my manic book-accumulation period, I acquired all the Reprints, includ-ing the eight volumes of Arber's Garner, and, of course, the great Stanyhurst was among them. This volume survived the disappearance of my first library, and after the war I was able to introduce Dylan to its delights. He was highly amused by some of Stanyhurst's expressions: 'the well-known sea', 'the brownye lion', 'draftye poetrye', 'Hesperides Sinagog', 'cocknye dandiprat hopthumb'; and by his descriptions:

---

* *Quite Early One Morning* (Dent, 1954).

(Dido's anger): 'Shall a stranger give me the slampam?'
(Courtiers' applause): 'The Troians plaudite flapped'
(Romantic passage): 'Dido and thee Troian captayne doo
      iumble in one den,
    And Nymphs in mountains high typ doe squeak, Hullelo,
    yearning'.

I put forward to Dylan my theory that while hexameters may work after a fashion in some foreign languages, for example in Goethe's *Hermann und Dorothea*, they seem always to drive poets writing in English mad, in the direction either of the absurdly prosaic or of the crazily fantastic. To prove my point, I showed him Longfellow's *Evangeline* and *Miles Standish*, Kingsley's *Andromeda* and Clough's *The Bothie of Tober-na-Vuolich*. Dylan urged me to write a half-hour script on the subject and persuaded Aneirin to fall in with the idea. I called the script 'Barbarous Hexameters' (a quotation from Tennyson), and arranged it so that I had to read all the link passages, which, by the way, included an account of the sinister life of Stanyhurst himself, while Dylan was given the quotations. My part, of course, was easy: I had merely to keep a straight face and read in a matter-of-fact voice. Dylan's part in reading the quotations, on the other hand, demanded the greatest virtuosity. He was in excellent form, and we recorded straight away without a re-take. Two examples will show the kind of thing Dylan had to face in this performance:

> JONES   When Stanyhurst wants to achieve an onomatopoeic effect, his favourite trick is to hyphenate two words.
> THOMAS   Flush-flash clush-clash ruffe-raffe muff-maff crack-rack tag-rag wig-wag rip-rap kym-kam rif-raf swish-swash thwick-thwack robble-hobble.

Stanyhurst's storm scene: *

> THOMAS   These flaws theyre cabbans with stur snar jarrye doe ransack,
> Like bandog grinning, with gnash tusk greedelye snarring,

* The 'g' in 'gnash' to be pronounced.

78

Like wrastling meete winds with blaste contrarius huzing,
Where curs barck bawling, with yolp yalpe snarrye rebound-
    ing,
A sea-belch grounting on rough rocks rapfully frapping.

Dylan read all this magnificently, and, as I said, all went well. The chief danger, of course, was that we would spoil the recording by laughing out aloud; the script had to be 'put over' in a strictly straight-faced manner, of course. The danger was at its greatest when Dylan pronounced the words 'Miles Standish' in the following quotation; at that point he suddenly turned to me and, standing stiffly to attention, saluted smartly, just as if I were Priscilla the Puritan maid herself:

So I have come to you now, with an offer and proffer of marriage
Made by a good man and true, Miles Standish the Captain of
Plymouth!

I still, of course, have the script of 'Barbarous Hexameters', and the recording was duly broadcast, but when I asked about the tape itself I was told that it was lost. This seems a pity for two reasons: it was the only broadcast made by Dylan and myself for which I wrote the script, and, in any case, I think it was funny. Perhaps the tape will turn up somewhere unexpectedly one day.

To turn from radio to television: by chance, I was present during Dylan's first performance in this medium; Fred Janes, John Prichard and I took part in it with him. It was the first time for all of us, and each hid from the others his secret apprehensions. To cushion ourselves against these we took even more than the usual amount of refreshment in one of the Cardiff pubs near the place of trial. The programme was not well planned by present-day standards; if the producer reads these words I hope he will forgive me for saying so. Instead of devising some sort of mingling of the participants, at least for part of the time, the producer had decided that each of us should do his own 'little piece'. Fred, John and I decided to prepare in advance only a vague outline of topics; apart from sticking to this, we thought it best to make our contributions extempore. This was not Dylan's plan. While the rest of us chatted and laughed nervously, Dylan covered the backs of several envelopes with his tiny handwriting. His eyes were glazed; he remained silent, but occasionally chuckled. All he would tell us was that his piece was about a certain Mrs Parsnip.

The testing time came. Fred, John and I acquitted ourselves without distinction but without shame. Dylan, as the star turn, was reserved for the last. Swinging his short legs, he sat on the studio table, his neck swelling, his face getting redder and redder in the hot lights as the camera 'zoomed in'. We all expected something amusing, and so it was. Unfortunately, the humour of the piece depended on manipulation of words, and, of course, they should have been properly memorized. All went well at first, but by the slipping of some ratchet of word-memory Dylan suddenly found himself at the beginning again, and, to our horror, we heard a repeat; then, at the same point, the same thing happened. I was reminded of something that may happen to reindeer when crossing a fjord; if the leader gets behind the tail of the herd, the animals will swim round and round in circles until they drown. The studio manager began to make frantic rotatory gestures, but instead of winding up, Dylan wound round. Towards the end of the third repeat, 'I had a landlady called Mrs Par . . .' Snip! Dylan's camera light went out, and the monitors showed an announcer who, wincing but with a forced smile, rounded off the programme.

This was the inauspicious beginning of a very short television career that was, it must be said, unsuccessful. I saw Dylan on television two or three times later, but never with a feeling of comfort. What was wrong? If I closed my eyes, everything was fine. Perhaps, unlike children, Dylan was to be heard, not seen. If I opened my eyes, I was immediately struck by the intensity of the effort Dylan was making to project himself. This is the sort of technique that can be very successful in public, before an audience. But even a professional actor whom we have just seen performing splendidly before the camera may, when interviewed on television about his acting or himself, become embarrassingly inarticulate or uncomfortably artificial. The same tricks will not do in front of the treacherous television camera lens.

Dylan would, of course, have realized this if he could have seen himself, as he had so often heard himself from radio tapes. In any case, with experience, he might have learned how to handle the medium. But there was no time.

7

Overmilk'd Wood

The myth of Dylan Thomas was born when the man, Dylan, died. But labour pains made themselves felt just before that birth. While Dylan lay in a coma, as soon as it became fairly clear that he would not survive, that is, when there was little danger that the living man would disconcertingly turn up somewhere to confront people and bear witness to the truth about himself, those who cared not a hoot for him, who barred him their homes, offered him no help, no money, looked upon him as a dishonest, drunken waster, began to wring their hands and cry to the heavens, 'A Genius is taking his leave of us!' Under different circumstances, the situation would have had its comic side, as in a scene from Jonson or Molière.

Some people, of course, enjoy grief; there are some, too, who take pleasure in observing the grief of others. One of this kind troubled to walk all the way from the centre of Swansea up the precipitous slope of Constitution Hill to call on me at Rosehill Terrace, where I then lived, in order to get me alone with himself in a room and announce, while concentrating his gaze on my face, and especially my eyes, 'Dylan Thomas is ill, very ill, probably dying.' I kept my face absolutely motionless, without a twitch, and, I hope, there wasn't even a flicker in my eyes. I hardly knew the self-appointed messenger, and saw to it that he gained no satisfaction for his pains. But he was only the first of a long series that was to extend far into future years, the series of uninvited visitors who called on Dylan's account.

In the week before Dylan's illness, a local newspaper had published an article that tore his works to pieces and consigned

82

them and him to the ash-heap. Immediately after his death, that is, within a fortnight of the previous issue, the same paper printed an article praising Dylan's work to the skies; a Homer, a Shakespeare, a Goethe all rolled into one had been lost to us. Even more extravagant were the references to Dylan as a person; for example, he was described as 'one of Nature's gentlemen.' *One of Nature's gentlemen!* That was exceptionally rich. The mythologizing had begun.

At first I did not realize what was happening. The Estate consisted solely of debts; my mind was occupied with my duties as Literary Trustee and with anxiety about the welfare of the Thomas family. At the same time, all who were closely concerned with Dylan, his work and his family, seemed to suffer in varying degrees from a kind of hysteria. I myself was not excluded from this. In spite of my outward calmness and artificial, newly acquired business-like air, I was really in as unstable a condition as many of the most hysterical around me. This showed itself in various forms of exaggeration: excessive punctiliousness in the execution of what I considered my duties, jealousy in the preservation of texts, suspicion of others, and irritability in my relations with them. I was suddenly plunged into an environment unfamiliar to me, the environment of broadcast drama and the theatre; it would not be too much to say that at one period I quarreled with all around me on the slightest cause, not realizing that they too were suffering from nerves and were really exercising some restraint in dealing with me.

Gradually the public was drawn into an awareness of tragedy, need, and work to be perpetuated. Funds were organized, both here and across the Atlantic; quite quickly the necessary money was accumulated. But symptoms of the growth of a myth accompanied all this activity. It was seriously proposed that the money accumulated by one Fund should go to the erection of a colossal statue of the poet on a Welsh cliff looking out over the sea. Memorial readings and performances blossomed all over London, the actors giving their services with the generosity characteristic of their profession; people declaimed 'And death shall have no dominion' at the Dominion Theatre. Everyone was asking, 'But what was *he* like?' The infant Dylan myth was well nurtured by the remarks, comments and hints of those who did not know the answer.

I can dismiss my own part in this with a few words. My work as Literary Trustee, which was, of course, unpaid, proved to be heavy and time-consuming. The correspondence ranged through all degrees from the imbecilic to the penetrating. Everything had to be answered, but the serious correspondence took up most energy and time. Some queries demanded careful thought and investigation, followed by the laborious composition of answers that might occupy several hours. There was no time for my own work, and in any case I had no thought or energy to spare for it. At the end of two years my own family was almost in as great need as the Thomas family had been at the time of Dylan's death. The Thomas Estate, on the contrary, was now like a ship well-launched and sailing always faster before a freshening wind. It was time for me to resign, and I did.

This resignation, which I thought would mark the end of persecution, was only its beginning. I expected a continuation of correspondence, and I simply passed most of it on to the right quarter. But there remained some correspondence addressed to me personally, not as a trustee, and it was for me to deal with it, or ignore it. The postage stamp usually showed the head of George Washington, and the contents varied from queries about Dylan's personal hygiene to questions about his knowledge of the *Rig Veda*. Sometimes the academic aims of the writer were mentioned, an M.A. or a Ph.D., perhaps. Sometimes the writer left it entirely to me what I replied about Dylan Thomas: anything, anything. I remember particularly an American lady whom I neglected right up to the end. In despair, she took to sending me drawings. Her last drawing was on a postcard: it was of a Hecuba-like woman, kneeling, with dishevelled hair, hands and eyes upraised imploringly, with tears pouring down her cheeks to collect in a pool around her

84

3. Opposite The White Hart, Llanddarog, Autumn 1951
Dylan Thomas, Daniel Jones, Dylan Jones
(Photograph taken by Irene Jones)

knees; underneath, in large capitals were printed the words: 'ANYTHING IN WRITING ABOUT DYLAN THOMAS! I BEG! I IMPLORE!' This appeal melted even my stony heart, and I sent her a card congratulating her on her draughtsmanship, which, after all, was good.

Then the unannounced visits to my house began. It was assumed that I would be delighted to discuss Dylan Thomas, the man and his work, but particularly the man, for hours on end with perfect strangers at any time of day or night, casting my own work or leisure on one side. Late one evening, for example, I was sitting in warmth and comfort with my feet up thoroughly enjoying some rubbish on television, when the doorbell rang. Opening the door, I found a group of strangers crowded together in the porch and even on the threshold. There seemed to be lots of them; those at the back craned their necks and stood on tiptoe, and all gawked. Eventually the leader spoke. 'We're from Blanksville, on our way to Laugharne, and thought we'd drop in for a chat about Dylan Thomas.'

On another occasion I was returning to the house from a walk 'thinking of nothing much', when I was treated to a surprise. I was reminded of a time when, on turning the corner of a country lane, I came suddenly upon a five-barred gate which was being used as a perch by about twenty turkeys; they all stared at me without moving, fixedly, meaninglessly. Now, the approach to my door consists of a winding series of wide, deep steps. Turning in at the gate, I was suddenly confronted with about twenty people sitting on these steps, at different heights and angles; all motionless, and all staring at me as if they were gazing into the infinite vacuity of space beyond the furthest galaxies. At length the withered brown dewlap of one of them quivered, and the syllables grated slowly out: 'Die . . . lan Thom . . . as . . .' No light came into the eyes, but perhaps the vacuum into which they gazed was not a vacuum at all; perhaps there gleamed in it here and there the mirage of a Ph.D. diploma.

4.   The Two Dylans, Jones (standing on the window-sill) and Thomas, outside 22 Rosehill Terrace, Swansea, Spring 1951
(Photograph taken by Irene Jones)

My Friend Dylan Thomas

To describe the innumerable similar visits I was privileged to receive would tire you almost as much as they tired me. But I must remove the danger of a possible misunderstanding. It is true that about three quarters of the visitors I have decribed were American, while other nationalities made up the remaining quarter. In spite of this, and in spite of much provocation, I feel no resentment towards intruders on the grounds of their nationality alone; that would be silly. Many Americans come to this country every year for various reasons, when they can afford or have facilities to do so; though numbering thousands, they constitute a very small proportion of their population. Of this small proportion only a still smaller proportion takes the trouble to intrude on my privacy, and I must remind myself that some of these, merely brash and insolent to all appearances, are really acting in a spirit of childlike simplicity, quite unaware of the extreme annoyance and inconvenience they cause. On such small grounds, it would be quite illogical to harbour any resentment against Americans as a whole.

I learned fairly quickly not to admit my uninvited visitors into the house. In the first place, admission involved a much greater waste of time. But there was another reason for my lack of hospitality, a sinister one; I hasten to say that this does not apply to Americans. Very often the visitors were shown into the front room and left alone there until I joined them from my study upstairs. In this front room, a fairly large one, I kept the bulk of what I think of as my third library. After a time I noticed that certain books were missing, particularly from the Dylan Thomas section. Many of them were, of course, first editions, and others rare and probably valuable. Twenty years before, in the days of my wonderful first library, this would have broken my heart, but the painful loss of that library, through friendly rather than enemy action, had taught me a kind of stoicism. My only regret was the disappearance of the first printing of *Llareggub*, in Botteghe Oscure, volume XIII, and even then my regret was more than half due to the fact that I knew with absolute certainty who took it.

86

Unfortunately, almost every house contains a very useful gadget that can be used as a means of access by an intruder, even when doors are bolted and barred: the telephone. I give two examples of typical 'phone calls; they should be enough.

(1) Ring. 'Daniel Jones?' 'Yes; who is it?' 'You wouldn't know me but . . .' 'Let's come to the point. What do you want to know about Dylan Thomas?' 'Well, I thought we could have a get-together, in a pub perhaps, for a little chat about him; you like a drink, I expect (hearty laugh). I'm not a Drinking Man myself, but the drinks would be on me . . .' Click. Ring. 'Sorry. We were cut off. I . . .' 'Yes, I know we were. *I* cut us off, like this . . .' Click.

(2) (To appreciate the richness of the following one-sided conversation, it must be explained that I live in a part of Swansea a good five miles from the centre of the city, where The Dragon Hotel stands.) Ring. American lady, breathless but business-like: 'Daniel Jones? I'm on my way to Laugharne and am at The Dragon. I can fit you in half-an-hour to talk about Dylan Thomas if you come at once. Time's a-wastin'.' Click (*my* click).

Outside the house, of course, I am easy prey. Sometimes I have a genuine desire not to displease; for example, a friend might buttonhole me and say, 'I have an American girl staying with me, charming girl; she's dying to meet you to talk about Dylan Thomas; I'll bring her along.' What answer can I give, since this is a friend who is speaking?

Some circuitous approaches are very amusing; they are of different types. One of the most subtle is through music. 'You don't know me, but may I congratulate you on your last broadcast? Most interesting; I'd like to discuss it with you. I have a few friends with me, if you wouldn't mind joining us for a minute. This is X, this Y, this Z. Yes, what was I saying? Oh, congratulations . . .' The congratulations die away to silence, and I begin counting inwardly, 'One, two, three, four . . .' About the count of eight, it comes: 'I understand you were a great friend of Dylan Thomas.'

My Friend Dylan Thomas

Another approach is through the 'Old School'. 'Hello.' 'Hello.' I look up and see someone who might or might not be a stranger, with a face that could be anybody's. There seem to be some dark figures behind him, about three feet away. 'You remember me, of course: Ianto ap Edwards, of 3A.' (3A was the class of at least a thousand pupils, one of whom was Dylan.) 'Grunt.' 'You see, you see,' Ianto turns to his companions, 'I told you he'd know me.' The cronies creep nearer. 'You remember when we used to go to the pub: Ifor, *Dylan*, you, Gwilym, *Dylan*, Maldwyn, *Dylan* and I . . . what a laugh!' To the cronies, who are now crowding round: 'You see! I told you!'

Such experiences are strange enough, but the most extra-ordinary occasions have been those when I have heard accounts of episodes I know are true, because Dylan and I were the chief protagonists in them, the only difference being that the chief protagonists have now become Dylan and the narrator.

My reactions at such times have given me the reputation of a crosspatch, a kodiak with a megrim;* and I must confess that my atrabilious night-thoughts sometimes run along the lines: 'Was it worth it? Any of it?' Without clarifying what this self-searching may imply, I will simply say that the light of dawn always brings me to the sane conclusion, 'Yes, it *was* worth it.'

But I was not always surly with people who approached me about Dylan Thomas. To tell the truth, my curiosity about the myth began to be aroused to such an extent that it sometimes overcame my irritation. In a pub one evening, a stranger sat next to me and began without introduction to ply me with questions about Dylan. I answered every one of them politely and as well as I could. He then got up and prepared to take his leave, not without saying, 'Thanks; I've enjoyed our chat.' But I caught hold of him by the sleeve and made him sit down again. 'The conversation has been too one-sided. You've asked

---

* Biggest bear, worst headache.

questions and I've replied. Would you mind answering some
questions of mine?' 'Well, fair enough, I suppose.' 'Which is
your favourite Dylan Thomas poem?' Silence. A dim look came
into his eyes, not, I'm afraid, the look of one who with painful
difficulty weighs the merits of one of many choices against
another. A horrible suspicion arose in my mind. 'Have you read
any of his poetry?' 'Well, poetry's not much in my line.' 'Prose,
then. You know: "Nicole, bring me my slippers and give me my
nightcap." That's prose.' 'Sounds pretty queer to me.' 'It was
written by a Frenchman. You have to make allowances. Well?'
'Not that, either. But they say he was wonderful on the radio
and made some great discs. Our local society's always doing his
stuff.' 'Ah, you've heard them, attended the readings?' 'No.
But they say this Thomas was a great lad. A real Bohemian.
Went about in rags, always drunk, spewed blood, heaps of
women (nudge), died young, of drink, in a hotel in New York I
think. He was famous. Why, in our town we have a street called
Dylan Villas, and a caff called The Dylan Waffle, where you can
get an Under-milk-shake, which is one of his writings, you
know.'

This occasion, I must admit, marks one abysmal extreme. I
was luckier on other occasions; when, for example, in answer to
the question about Dylan's poetry, my new-found acquaintance exclaimed with some indignation, 'Of course! I can even
quote a line. Let me see. "And death shall have no dominion."
Or is that from the Bible, like "The mills of God"?'

I have thought a great deal about the Dylan myth; at its worst,
as my investigations seemed to suggest, it has little to do with
his work, and not even very much to do with him as he really
was. Romanticizing and mythologizing have much in common;
but they are different. The first emphasizes exaggeration, the
second distortion. The murderer Heath used to write in hotel
registers 'Group Captain Rupert Brooke'; no one, however
unstable, would think of adopting as his signature 'Vice-
Marshal Dylan Thomas'. The less historical fact available, the
better both romanticizing and mythologizing can flourish;

there is all the more manoeuvering space for the first to exaggerate and for the second to distort. Brooke, whose insipid verse leaves the impression of an indeterminate character, was known in school-books and associated with the '14-18 War, during which he died, not in action, but of a mysterious infection aboard a ship off Lemnos. This left plenty of scope for the romantic. Wilfred Owen, whose verse, perhaps the greatest anti-war poetry ever written, leaves a strong personal impression, died in action a few days before the end of the '14-18 War while heroically trying to lead his men across a river. All this is too precise. Then there is the aura that seems to surround some names, for example T. E. Lawrence, inviting exaggeration and distortion, while the same aura is not to be found about the figures of Hopkins, Yeats, Joyce, Eliot; informed study of the texts has given no opportunity for the aura to take shape.

Of course, I am not competent to discuss theories about the creation of gods and their myths, but, like any general reader, I get the impression that the animist Müller-Frazer theory has predominated for many years. However, I do happen to know that there is another theory, put forward by Lyall and Ridgeway, that challenges it.* Not always, but sometimes, they suggest, the cause is to be found not in symbolism of natural processes, but in lives of real men and women who have performed remarkable deeds in the past. People remember these deeds inaccurately, and, as time goes on, are apt to supplement them with inventions often prompted unconsciously by personal desires. This process is quite natural in a society with few or no historical records; in other words, historical accuracy has an effect directly contrary to mythologizing. At the same time, awe and dread must surround the legend, in order to give it religious force; for example, the hero, like young Adonis, must meet death before his time, and tragically. ''Twas only fear first in the world made gods.'

* William Ridgeway: *The Dramas and Dramatic Dances of Non-European Races* (C.U.P. 1915 pp. 125 ff.)

It is clear that all the conditions most favourable for mythologizing are present in the 'mystery' of Dylan's reputed character, life, and death. There is plenty of room for manoeuvre here. Out of this imaginary clay anything can be made to the desire of the moulder: a Bacchanalian, an Evangelist, an inspired madman, a martyr, a reincarnation of the Celtic past. The ungodlike word 'Thomas' has disappeared from 'Dylan Thomas' for a long time now in the Welsh press; as plain 'Dylan', resonant, but with a hint of intimacy, the word evokes all the ancient solemnity and rites of the Gorsedd, to which the real Dylan never belonged. According to legend, his appearance, even on the most casual occasions, only thinly veiled the arcane workings of creativity. A nincompoop once described to me his only meeting with Dylan: 'He allowed me to do all the talking. Leaning with one elbow on the bar counter, he raised his eyes to the ceiling; they were slightly glazed, and I knew that, undisturbed by my words, genius was even then at work in him.' I did not mention in reply that I knew well what that glazed look meant; it meant, 'how much can I "touch" this bloody bore for?'

But the most striking examples of 'moulding to the heart's desire' are to be found in the posthumous portraits. It is perhaps my bad luck that I have seen not one that resembles the original. There are two main types. In the first, based on photographs, the receding hair is brought forward, the forehead by way of compensation heightened, lips and nostrils narrowed, arms rounded, body unsexed, and fingers tapered as a musician's are supposed to be (but aren't). The second, based somehow on the poetry, creates a more rarefied impression; in the murk one can eventually make out a darker gibbosity pierced by a couple of bilious spots: this is Dylan by owl-light, and it has, I am sure, much symbolic significance.*

In the context of the Dylan legend the controversial subject

* The best portrait of Dylan is a very fine picture by Alfred Janes in the National Museum of Wales, Cardiff; it was painted during Dylan's lifetime, when he was about eighteen years old.

of his influence cannot, of course, be avoided. As I see it, this influence has three aspects: encouragement to write, imitation of style, and partial occultation of the 'artistic scene'.

Dylan was for a time a reporter on a provincial paper. How many reporters on provincial papers have imagined themselves to be corporals with batons hidden in their scratch-pads? How many junior announcers have dropped their voices a major sixth? All of them, reporters and announcers, thinking to themselves, of course, 'If Dylan could "make it" why can't I?'

In my opinion, and as far as I know, the influence of Dylan on his imitators has been uniformly bad. Of course, many artists, fine in themselves, have exercised a bad influence. Murillo, Victor Hugo and Wagner, for example, are 'acknowledged masters'; but the direct action of their work, as opposed to the reaction against it, has resulted in achievements of dubious quality. It is a trite observation, but it must be said that the essence that confers their status on such artists cannot be reproduced, while everything that is marginal, the mannerisms and superficies of style, can be imitated. The more strongly flavoured the style, the easier the imitation.

Here I am on dangerous ground. I have undertaken to make no direct comment on Dylan's work. But within these self-imposed limits, I can still say this: Maupassant, for example, is a writer very difficult, if not quite impossible to imitate; Dylan was not a writer of this type; in fact, he was different in the extreme. A multiplicity of adjectives is a characteristic of his imaginative prose style, and this is one of the respects in which he has had too many imitators. Sometimes I wish that there hung on the walls of every broadcasting studio and newspaper office in Wales Flaubert's warning: 'The adjective is the enemy of the noun.' Whole shiploads of potential writers have sunk into oblivion beneath the waves of Dylan's 'style', (that is, marginal characteristics), with the result that the question has been asked, and asked seriously, 'Has Dylan Thomas ruined Anglo-Welsh literature?' My answer to this would be 'No', because there are still many writers who have stood firm against the Influence. Where are they? Who are they? This brings me to my third point.

I ask the reader to imagine himself at the theatre seated behind a very fat lady, wearing a very large hat, who keeps talking very loudly. He can be only vaguely aware that there is some activity on the stage; only a confused sound of voices comes to him. The lady represents Dylan's work and his myth, the stage, the place where other Welsh artists persevere in their work, artists who have the ability and the originality to maintain independence at the cost of comparative neglect. For this occultation of Welsh art by his work and his myth, Dylan himself, of course, is in no way to blame, any more than those on the stage are responsible for the presence of the fat lady. It would be Dylan's hope and the 'actors'' hope that the theatre-goer has the sense simply to change his seat and view things from a different angle.

Much in this chapter is controversial, but none of it is intentionally provocative. Two points must be made clear: the limits of the reading, or non-reading public for whom my remarks are intended, and the reason why I think those remarks, derogatory and ironical as some of them are, are necessary.

Wherever English is spoken, and in some places where it is not, Dylan's work has its following of admirers. They value it with sanity and discrimination. Their critical faculty is not asleep, and faults are not overlooked; their appreciation, when it is aroused, is genuine and significant. They show no tendency to surround with a mystic aura either the man or his work. These, of course, are the readers whose opinions Dylan himself would prize. Perhaps I owe an apology to them, and should explain that my tetchy sallies have not been aimed in their direction.

At the same time, I have felt it necessary to write this chapter, even at the risk of being misunderstood.

It is not irrelevant to mention here a B.B.C. script I wrote many years ago, called 'Handel versus Handelianism'; I well recall the trouble it caused. Dismayed by the ill-treatment of a few well-known works of this composer, and outraged by the neglect of others, I took it upon myself to defend the great man from his 'cult'. After the broadcast, my post-bag was heavy. One correspondent wrote to this effect: 'You decry Handel. Beethoven admired him. Whose opinion should we value, yours or Beethoven's?' This came from someone who had at least listened to the broadcast; in my script I had mentioned Beethoven's admiration for Handel, and I am fairly sure that the writer would not otherwise have known about it. In the rest of my correspondence there was a general agreement, apparently based on hearsay, that I had actually attacked Handel's music; implicit in this assumption was probably the idea that a contemporary composer could take up no other position.

In this chapter I have tried to defend Dylan against Dylanism and to avoid, if possible, the kind of misunderstanding I have just described. My aim was to remove foolish adulation from the writings and foolish mythologizing from the writer. I had to lay the ghost to raise up the man; this would have Dylan's approval, I think. Dylan did not like himself very much; he would have liked his myth even less. Least of all, he would have liked his influence.

8

After the Fight

Throughout this book I have tried deliberately to hide myself from the reader in order to keep his whole attention upon Dylan. Now it is no longer any use concealing the fact that I have been present all the time. Dylan has been kept in the centre of the stage, but only under my direction, through my opinions. How much do I really know? What entitles me to present opinion as knowledge? These are what people call 'good' questions: in other words, questions it would be more comfortable to ignore.

I have repeatedly been called Dylan's 'best friend'. When these words have been used in my presence I have never made any comment, not because I necessarily disagree, but because I find it too difficult to make any comment at all. Perhaps 'best friend' is roughly the right description; perhaps not. I certainly was Dylan's closest friend for the longest time, twenty-eight years. But if these words, 'closest', 'longest', are separated, by which of them can a relationship be measured? Certainly not by length of time. An intimate relationship maintained intermittently in the course of one month may be more significant than a superficial relationship continuing without interruption for several years. This throws all the responsibility for what I have written about Dylan in this book upon the quality of my relationship with him, and I must now try to describe what is perhaps indescribable.

Dylan himself gives an account of our first meeting and earliest year of friendship in his story *The Fight*.* This account

* In *Portrait of the Artist as a Young Dog* (Dent, 1940).

is accurate, though, of course, some of the names are altered. We did indeed begin our friendship with a fight. Dylan got a black eye, my nose bled, and no one was the winner. All this was quite normal. But Dylan calls the *whole* of our early friendship *The Fight*, not just the beginning of it, and this is remarkable. It is as if Dylan, with extraordinary insight or intuition, was aware of a continuing conflict between our natures. I can't remember what caused the fight, but it seems to me that no cause was needed. Perhaps Dylan's presence and my presence in the same place at the same time, these circumstances, and no others, simply marked the beginning of *The Fight*. Our natures, different as they were, complemented one another perfectly and formed an extraordinarily firm relationship in which, however faintly, there always lay hidden an element of opposition.*

But even this rather complicated view of the situation is not exactly accurate; perhaps it is misleading, and I must continue to try to explain it even if I run the risk of seeming to contradict myself. The truth is that the situation presented a paradox. We were at variance only on the periphery of our relationship; at its heart there remained, undisturbed, a harmony of thought and feeling that rarely exists between two human beings. Otherwise, our collaboration, our shared humour and experiences, and our continuous close friendship over so long a period, would have been impossible. It is this harmony that Dylan tried to express by fusing our names into one adjective: *Warmdandylanley.†*

The physical resemblance between us was slight; yet we were very often mistaken for brothers and even for one another: as far as I can see, there was no material reason for it. This is what I find so difficult, if not impossible to describe: the way in which

---

* Many complementary oppositions, roughly corresponding with Dylan's tendencies and mine, may occur to readers; for example, Dionysos (inspiration, excess) and Apollo (reason, order), Widdershins and Deisheal (against and with the sun's course).

† See the end of the second letter in Chapter 4: 'All the love of one WARMDANDYLANLEY-MAN to the other one.'

Dylan and I were virtually 'the same'. The difficulty is aggravated by the distance from which I am looking at our relationship as I write these words, because my own character has had plenty of time to change. In those days Dylan and I were like two ships riding at anchor, the same anchor, straining to sail apart, but remaining securely moored in the same place. One ship foundered, the other weighed anchor to sail away, and from the distance of twenty-three years, I find it hard to make out the place where the anchorage was shared.

One outstanding difference between Dylan and myself must by now be overpoweringly evident. I had, and went on having a tendency to be academic; Dylan's tendency was, of course, in the opposite direction. At the beginning of our first term at school we fought, and the physical encounter had a symbolic meaning. In the same first term, we confronted one another again, this time in a mental encounter, but in a similar way. An enterprising young student teacher took it into his head to organize a form debate. Dylan was to maintain that the contribution of contemporary poetry to literature far outweighed all contributions to literature of the past put together; I was to uphold the contrary view. I prepared my paper carefully, with the help of several reference books, and the result was a dull résumé of world literature from Homer to Browning, with occasional quotations. I ended by asking with heavy irony whether it was fair to expect the literary contribution of a single generation to surpass in value the combined contributions of so many centuries. When I sat down, I smugly felt that victory was in my pocket. I forgot then to ask myself how many boys had listened to me, and for how long, but, even now, I remember Dylan's speech quite well. It was remarkable in several different ways. I was struck, for example, by the fact that it had nothing to do with the subject. Not a single contemporary poet was mentioned, not a single line of poetry quoted. I could make out that the whole of the past, not just its literary aspect, was under attack; there was a mention of the ticklishness of periwigs on bald domes. The speech was well written and it was funny; everyone remained awake and there was occasional laughter. Dylan won easily on a show of hands. Ralph Hodgson's team beat Homer's; final score: the Hodgsons 35, the Homers nil.

I have already emphasized Dylan's concentration on one subject, English, and his refusal to submit himself to any form of discipline, whether imposed by himself or by others. In contrast, my own interest in mathematics and, particularly, in foreign languages, was genuine and not forced upon me by school discipline; out of school hours, for example, I tried to teach myself some foreign languages that were not in the school syllabus. Dylan and I, closest of friends, found ourselves at the opposite extremes in the form gradings. But I was not the swot and prig all this implies; I no more knelt before the general Oppressor, School, than Dylan did. My notes on Ovid's *Metamorphoses*, for example, were written in an ink of my own invention, with the result that the exercise-book eventually turned into a solid block of wood; at the same time, in some way not immediately connected with school tuition, my performance in Latin was not affected, perhaps because I was simply interested in it. Though not as often as Dylan, I did my share of 'mitching'.* Our favourite trick on a fine morning was to turn in at the top gate of Cwmdonkin Park and spend hours together there, reading and writing poetry. And at University, I attended lectures more from choice than from a sense of duty; I was well aware that the standard of tuition was not uniformly high, and that certain hours could be more profitably spent in the library than in the lecture-room.

But, however hard I try to find a way of escape, I can't quite refute the charge that I had then, and perhaps still have a weakness for thinking in an academic fashion. Particularly in my immediate post-graduate years I bore my little learning very

---

* Playing truant, like 'playing mwchins' (*Under Milk Wood*). I thought this was a particularly South Walian expression until I read Iona and Peter Opie's *The Lore and Language of Schoolchildren* (1959, p. 372). They give it a wider distribution and an older history.

heavily. Dylan cried out once in protest, 'My God, Dan, I don't mind your quoting, but don't tell me the work, the author, the page and the publisher!' In those days I was thesis-minded and possessed by bibliomania. I think that Dylan's outburst did me good, and, apart from this, I went through the process of learning more, which gradually taught me how little I knew.

Another significant difference between Dylan and myself was our degree of sophistication. More than a year younger, he always seemed much older. For his 'sophisticated' interests he had other companions. M.L. was his partner in the strip-poker games at L's house; this at a time when I could understand the language of Juvenal's Sixth Satire better than its meaning. Almost every Sunday afternoon, when the pubs were closed, he played gin rummy for small stakes at The Mermaid with companions whom he probably met on no other occasion. With Bert Trick he discussed the plight of the proletariat. Later, fellow reporters, much older and tougher, introduced him to really hard drinking and the temptations of the 'Pink 'Un'.* Later still, not in the Soho Wheatsheaf days but in the B.B.C. Gluepot days, Dylan would sometimes converse with friends in a language that seemed to me to be in code.† Any contribution I ventured to make would meet with a shocked silence, as if a dumb man were suddenly to declaim a Hamlet soliloquy at the top of his voice; my words, I felt, were not in the right language.

But before I speak directly about the Dylan-Dan relationship, I must deal with a much simpler subject: the ordinary circumstances of life that sometimes had the effect of bringing us together and sometimes parted us. I have already described the 'Warmley days'. Dylan's transition from schoolboy to reporter was imperceptible, and made no difference to our contact. He was now even in a position to support a scheme Tom Warner and I hatched out together: nothing less than a

* Affectionate term for *The Sporting Times*, which specialized in racing information.
† Wheatsheaf: a pub in Rathbone Place, off Oxford Street. Gluepot: The George, near Langham Place.

My Friend Dylan Thomas

Swansea Symphony Orchestra! Far more than our share of sly advertisement for this venture appeared in the *Evening Post* above the initials D.M.T. People started calling at Warmley. There was a short, fat man with a waxed moustache who played piccolo duets with his friend, a tall saturnine character; these duets all had bird titles, like 'The Lark and the Nightingale'. There was one candidate who played the trumpet so badly that I was physically sick; I had to leave the audition to Tom, and my moans could be heard from the bedroom curiously mingled with the trumpeter's odd mooings. We had a composer, yes, a composer; a lady who had written tunes for us to elaborate, harmonize, develop, construct, orchestrate and perform: that's all. Her name was Greeba Tynte, which, as names go, has, I think, a slight edge on *Runia Tharp*.*

But I must remind myself that my subject is the way in which Dylan helped us at the *Evening Post* offices. For example, when the S.S.O. was badly in need of bassoonists, Dylan gave us a big banner in the *Post*, followed by an impassioned plea in elaborately ornate language; surely, he argued, there must lurk within the confines of Cwmbwrla some Attic warbler versed in this tricksy, frisky instrument? The appeal brought an immediate reply from someone in the Uplands. Tom and I rushed to meet this *rara avis*, who turned out to be a lank, swarthy man, living testimony to the truth of the theory that musicians grow to resemble the instruments they play. He had a puzzled look on his face. 'Yes, I play the bassoon. But there's something I want to know. It's about the chap who wrote that piece in the *Evening Post*. My wife doesn't like the instrument; how does he know that she won't let me practise it anywhere but in the attic?'

We had a lot of fun out of the S.S.O., and Dylan enjoyed giving us all the publicity he could; but nothing came of our schemes.

* The friend of Victor Neuberg mentioned by me in *Dylan Thomas: The Poems* (Dent, 1971, p. 258, note on Poem 79) and by Constantine FitzGibbon in *The Life of Dylan Thomas* (Dent, 1965, p. 106).

After the Fight

My contact with Dylan continued throughout my undergraduate years, but I saw a little less of him as time went on,
because of the increasing pressure of my work. His own work
seemed to be very sporadic or non-existent. Sometimes he
would sit in silence at one table, writing, while at another I
struggled with yet another of my interminable series of essays.
But often the silence would gradually become not so much a
silence as an absence of sounds, a vacuum which we were both
straining to fill; when this happened, Dylan would get up and
leave, promising to meet me for a drink in the evening.

After graduation, in spite of the fact that I had to work both
at the Royal Academy of Music and at the British Museum, I
saw a lot more of Dylan. It is true that I held a university
research scholarship, but the grant was small, and I was about as
poor as he was. Our situations were similar. We both had left
home, and everything that home meant in the way of
restriction and support; feeling free, and wildly so, we
cheerfully threw ourselves on our wits to find ways of carrying
on. Soho and Chelsea became our 'homes', and episodes of our
lives were like 'Scènes de la Vie de Bohème'. This really means
that we didn't know when we were going to eat or where we
were going to sleep, and didn't care.

But the reader would be mistaken in supposing that this sort
of existence was in any way 'romantic'. I always associate it
with a certain poet I got to know; I forget his name. Poet; or
sculptor? Which was he? He created enormous shapeless
sculptures. On the other hand, he persisted in writing five-act
blank verse historical plays with titles like *Clovis the Ninth,
Clothilde the Fourth, Dagobert the Thirteenth, Theophilus
Paleologus the Second.* One day he invited me back to his
studio in Chelsea, to stay the night, if I liked. The studio looked
and smelt like an enormous Victorian conservatory, an
abandoned one, and there were indeed ferns growing in the
corners. My feet got wet, crossing the floor: small tribute either
to the floor or to my shoes. During the day he chipped away,
either at chunks of stone or chunks of blank verse; that wasn't

so bad. But all night he worked at a pie factory; his job was to take steak-and-kidney pies from a moving belt and pack them in cardboard boxes. The belt travelled fast, a supervisor was constantly on the watch, and he hadn't time to snaffle one. He was starving, and the factory atmosphere, unlike the studio atmosphere, was very savoury. That, to me, represents the 'Romance' of Bohemianism.

Dylan and I, however, managed somehow. I eked out my grant, and a poem of his occasionally appeared in a periodical. He also had some reviewing to do, and kindly passed on to me what he called 'the heavy old stuff', that is, reviews of fairly academic books. When this happened, we shared the review fees, and afterwards sold the books themselves at a special place in the Strand, dividing the proceeds.

Then, suddenly, my situation was transformed. I won a valuable travelling scholarship, and at the same time was able to convince the university authorities that this would not conflict with my work for the research grant. I had to set out on my travels almost at once, and stay in various countries for a considerable time. It was impossible to maintain close contact with my friends, and I didn't try. On arrival in Paris, the first stage of my travels, I received a postcard of the Place de l'Opéra with the message: 'Wish you were here'; it had been sent by Dylan, Fred and Tom. This, I think, was my last contact with them until, much later, I returned from abroad. My two grants continued, and I was fairly well off, at least for a student. Now, instead of roaming from place to place, I settled in one spot, weighing myself down with the accumulation of objects. The objects I accumulated were chiefly books. Bibliomania had me firmly in its grip. I combed bookshops, first and second hand, attended auctions, advertised in *The Clique*, and brought together what I consider to have been a remarkable private library.

These, and other autobiographical details that must follow, cannot be avoided; they are necessary for an understanding of my contact with Dylan, at one time close, at another remote.

102

Our contact ceased, of course, during my stay abroad, and, though renewed, was not as close as it had been before, when I 'settled down' on my return. Separation again became complete when the war began and I was in the army. By intuition I knew that, whatever happened, Dylan would not be in the services; at the same time, like most other people then, I had no idea what would happen to me, and it seemed futile, if not impossible, to maintain a home in my absence. I lent Dylan my library and furniture for his studio in Manresa Road. In the meantime I went through a long course of training in the Royal Corps of Signals in various parts of England: contact with Dylan ceased at this time. Then someone noticed my linguistic qualifications on a form and I was transferred to the Intelligence Corps and sent first to Bedford and then to Bletchley. What went on in Bletchley is no longer an official secret; a book has been published on the subject.* I worked as a cryptographer first in the Italian-Rumanian, then in the Japanese Section.

I was now within visiting distance of London, and saw Dylan occasionally during short leaves. These encounters, in pubs, often necessarily at lunchtime, were far from satisfactory, as I shall describe later on. The period between the end of the war and my demobilization seemed interminable. At last, somewhere in Guildford, I was given a shirt, gaudily striped like pyjamas, a trilby hat two sizes too small, a pair of very tight trousers, and other tokens of civilian status. The hat I gaily threw from the lorry that took me away from the place, into a field for the cows to chew at; I don't remember what happened to the rest. But there was my gratuity, a large one, and I had to make up for years of enforced silence by writing a lot of music. I rented a cottage on the north coast of Cornwall, and to the howling of the wind against the thick stone walls wrote chamber music with furious speed and concentration. Contact with Dylan was again broken, this time for six months.

* F. W. Winterbotham: *The Ultra Secret* (Weidenfeld & Nicolson, 1974).

But both Dylan and I had to return to our native country; we were foreigners everywhere else. I went to Swansea and he went to Laugharne, but this made little difference. We saw one another very often; he always stayed with me in Swansea, I always stayed with him in Laugharne. We had returned to one another, in more ways than one, and this was the finest period in all our friendship.

I have postponed till now any direct discussion of my relationship with Dylan, because it was necessary first to give some outline of the circumstances, ordinary and boring as they might be, that chanced to bring us together or keep us apart.

People, speaking of friendship, often say: 'Our relationship remained perfectly constant. We took up where we left off, however long the period of absence.' I would not say this about my friendship with Dylan. For one thing, in the middle of its course, it sagged quite badly. For another, it was not the same friendship at the end as it had been in the beginning. I think of it as a relationship in three distinct stages.

The first stage has been described, or rather implied, in the earlier chapter about Warmley, and in the longer of the two letters from Dylan to me. But there is more to add about this period. We were then far more like brothers than friends. We thought and felt alike, but we were not the same, and not equal. I was conscious of Dylan's volatility and aware of his tendency to sudden unreasoning fury. My attitude, I suspect, was slightly tinged with fear; I felt sometimes, probably wrongly, that if I spoke out aloud what was really in my mind, this would end our friendship for ever. No one could be less tactful with other people than I was; yet with Dylan I sometimes felt it necessary to make an effort to adapt myself to him and to avoid dangerous areas. This attitude was not reciprocated by Dylan, who had his greater sophistication to help him; for example, without regard to my preferences, he tended to direct affairs, 'Now we'll write poetry', 'I'm tired of this; now we'll play cricket.' But the more subtle aspects of his attitude can only be conjectured. How profound was his loathing of the 'academic'?

Was he unconsciously jealous of my scholastic abilities? Did he resent the fact that, whereas I could enter into the whole of his world, he could enter only into a part of mine? Did he envy me the free-and-easy environment of my home? Instead of trying to answer these questions, I would rather leave them unanswered. I can say only that whatever the balance of give and take between us at this time, the interchange worked very successfully.

The second stage in our relationship was one I think of as 'the slump'. It would be easy to say that it lasted five or six years, that is, the period covering my army service and stay in Cornwall, but this would give a false picture. The absences did not matter; our encounters did. I would have been wise not to seek Dylan out at all during those short leaves from Bletchley. It was impossible to detach him from a new circle of acquaintances some of whom treated me with less than courtesy. Even my uniform seemed to provoke antagonism, an antagonism it would require only a little knowledge of psychology to understand. I wore uniform simply because I no longer had any civilian clothes. It would be impossible for me to look smart under any circumstances, but in my captain's uniform with shiny Sam Browne I came near enough to this to be at least awkwardly conspicuous in the groups surrounding Dylan.

On the other hand, I can see good reasons for the attitude of these acquaintances. Many of them were colleagues of Dylan's in his work, or were in some way related to it, and wished to discuss matters of interest only to themselves without the distraction of an outsider. Many asked themselves, 'Who is this Nobody who claims intimacy with a Somebody? Who is this man who speaks with such assurance about everything?' Some of these questions, for example the second, were well justified; I *did* have, and probably still have an annoying tendency to deliver lectures on almost all subjects. To make matters worse, some of my views were not fashionable at the time. I could not, for example, understand the general condemnation of Wagner's music, and my puzzlement made me bring up the matter more often than was welcome. I was introduced to Michael Ayrton with the words, 'This is the chap who actually *likes* Wagner.' To this I replied: 'I also like Couperin, Mussorgsky, Fauré, Johann Strauss Junior, and I have a surname, as well as a Christian name.' Such readiness to take offence and sharpness of reaction won me no new friends, and discussion with Dylan about me behind my back could not have done our relationship anything but harm.

At the same time, Dylan himself seemed different. He was now a famous man and often the centre of an admiring circle. I am ready to admit that in my feelings towards the closest of the sycophants there may have been a tinge of jealousy as I awkwardly shuffled about on the periphery of that charmed circle, but far stronger than this was the sense that Dylan had become remote. I suspect that if some proportion of the small amount of time I had for each London visit could have been spent alone with Dylan or with Dylan and two or three really close friends, any impression made on him by the insinuations of his new acquaintances would have vanished, and my feeling of the distance between us would have vanished too.

The third stage of our friendship was marked by our return to Wales. Is it too sentimental to suggest that this return to our native country meant also a return to our true selves? The third stage was not merely a renewal of our first relationship; it was the establishment of a new, better one. We had both, I think, gained from our experiences, and now were no longer brothers, but very close friends, equal in all respects, neither of us fearing or envying the other.

One of the most striking changes in Dylan was his new attitude to the 'academic'. This created yet another bond between us that had not existed before. I had at the time the grandiose scheme of writing a 'philosophy of music', and for three years had been intensively studying philosophical literature, some of which, I must admit, was only remotely related to my subject. In my study in Rosehill Terrace, Swansea, Dylan and I actually discussed this, and many other 'heavy old subjects'; a thing that would have been unthinkable ten years before. I remember, for example, that I had just read St Augustine's *De Ordine*, which seemed to lend support to my idea of God as the Principle of Order in the universe, and Dylan was so interested in the passages I translated for him that he copied them out. He examined my Chinese and Japanese books, and tried his hand at my own peculiar adaptation in English of the 'haiku' form, which may have attracted him because of its pattern based on the syllabic count (seventeen syllables).* The classification of all things on the earth and in heaven and the mind into two hundred and fourteen categories (the 'radicals') excited Dylan's wonderment, but, while admiring the beauty of the calligraphy, he was really interested only in ideographic characters: lid on woman for 'peace', two women in the same house for 'enmity', two moons in the same sky for 'friendship' (a rare phenomenon), and so on. This type of character attracted him because, he said, it embodied or suggested images.

The idea that Dylan could stomach such 'academic stuff', and still more the idea that it could interest him, was, as I have said, something entirely new. Constantine FitzGibbon tells us that Goronwy Rees was very astonished at Dylan's reply when he was asked towards the end of his life what his feelings would be if offered an honorary university degree: 'Dylan said at once that he would be delighted.'†

This close understanding between us lasted up to the moment of our final parting. It is odd now to think that that last meeting was due entirely to Dylan's insistence, and that, as a matter of fact, I tried to avoid it. At the time, I was working very hard to meet an almost impossible deadline, and when the

---

* I don't know what happened to Dylan's efforts, and therefore, with apologies, give one of my own:
    'In the Hall of Distorting Mirrors
    Suddenly some men look pleasant.'
† Constantine FitzGibbon: *The Life of Dylan Thomas* (Dent, 1965, p. 202).

telegram arrived, 'Must see you at Bush; on way to America', I thought, 'Just another of his trips over there', and went on working. In half-an-hour a taxi drew up outside the house, and Dylan shouted from it, 'Come on! come on! what's the matter with you?'

So began not one day, but nearly three days full of enjoyment and heavy with guilt. From time to time, Dylan read passages of *Under Milk Wood*, especially new ones, complete or incomplete, and spoke about his plans for finishing the work. I played him a recording of my third symphony, the last music of mine he heard; my next symphony was to be written in his memory.

But in the meantime we were both feeling the weight of our guilt more and more heavily. Dylan was getting later and later in fulfilling the travelling plans arranged for him, and gave a clear impression that he had no wish to go at all. I was getting later and later in meeting my deadline, and yet had no wish for Dylan to go. We both kept postponing our parting. Finally, on the morning of the last day, by some grim effort of will, I managed to get Dylan's packed suitcases as far as Ralph the Books' shop.* From there we went to several pubs, ending up at The Bush, where we drank until afternoon closing-time. We were now very hungry, and crossed the road to Cresci's for something-and-chips. There was a big clock on the wall, and as the hands moved steadily towards the time of Dylan's train I saw his eyes follow them. I read his thoughts perfectly. 'I am *not* going to catch that train. I am determined to be *too late* to catch it. There's always tomorrow.' Again I found strength somehow. I ran to Ralph's, seized the cases, ran back to Cresci's and propelled Dylan to the station. The train was just about to leave. As the train moved off, I started first walking, then running to keep up with it. Dylan stood at the open window, waving one hand slightly with exaggerated weakness and smiling an odd little smile. It was, in a sense, the last time I ever saw his face.

* The late Ralph Wishart, a great friend of ours.

108

9

Dylan and his Fetch

Like most people, I often make the casual claim that I 'understand' someone. Given the opportunity to find out a little more, I nearly always have to admit that I am wrong in several different ways: I am wrong in the presumption of my claim, in my 'conclusions', and in my failure to know enough. How can anyone ever know enough about a character? About one's self, for example? It's an impossibility, of course. On the other hand, some aspects of the subject can be discussed, and there is always a feeling, however mistaken, that the truth is somewhere, and is getting nearer.

One apparently reasonable question is this: are some characters more complex than others? It seems to me that Dylan's character, for example, was among the more complex rather than the less complex. I may discuss things of this kind without weakening my intention to reach no 'conclusion', because, in spite of them, I still cling to my belief that no 'conclusions' about people are possible.

The complexity of Dylan's character was due to the disharmony of his interior world and the exterior world, a disharmony at first perhaps forced on him, but later deliberately maintained. The long letter from Dylan which I have quoted fully earlier in the book proves how deliberate that intention was. He makes clear that his decision is not mere introversion or escapism. He asserts that the inner world is 'much more real' and 'much more worth while', but he goes significantly further than this: the outer world is 'only the setting for a world of your own' and the artist — Dylan means himself — should inhabit a secret inner world 'under the world-of-the-others'.

Detachment implies coldness, yet Dylan, onlooker as he was, was not a cold one. He was able to love and to move other people to love him; in fact, he craved affection. But 'outside there', that is, outside the place where he lived in hiding, things were images, and perfect relationships were possible only for those who never met, like Mog Edwards and Myfanwy Price. Dylan observed, not with a stony face, but with a melancholy smile, for he was a sad man. He said to me once: 'Everything is fine, except myself.'

The only ideal he clung to was an ideal possible to achieve only in childhood: the child-life itself. He wished to remain as a child, not to grow up, not to have to face 'realities', to be cosy, shut the world out, live from day to day, always with new 'excitements', clamouring like a child, 'What shall we do next? What shall we do next?' All this hovered before his mind like a mirage, and he was sick with nostalgia for the days when he was 'young and easy'.

Life does not permit anyone with such ideas and such ideals to be anything but chronically unhappy. Dylan's unhappiness has led many to believe that he suffered from a 'death-wish'. I disagree. There is a difference between a feeling of doom and a wish for death. When Dylan went on his last visit to America, he expected to return and he wished to return; one of his last acts in Swansea was to order his children's Christmas annuals from Ralph the Books. It was not a wish for death but a feeling of doom that oppressed him, a feeling his last photographs show in his eyes.

One expects a recluse to remain in his cell, a stylobite on top of his pillar, someone hiding to remain out of sight, not even showing himself in a mirror. But Dylan's life presented an extraordinary paradox. While remaining hidden, he sent into the world a counterfeit image of himself, a fetch.* This other

---

* This good English word may not be as familiar as the Latin *alter ego* or the German *Doppelgänger*, but at least it is not so pedantic. The idea occurs often in literature, for example in Conrad's *The Secret Sharer*.

Dylan became a part of the outer 'setting for the world of his own', Dylan's 'much more real and worth-while world under the world-of-the-others'. The counterfeit was accepted by many as the one and only Dylan Thomas, and it has a corresponding degree of importance or unimportance. In any case, I must try to describe the fetch, 'Dylan'.

In the first place, he coincided extraordinarily with the expectations and the wishes of those who met him. Chameleon-like, this Dylan adapted himself perfectly to his surroundings and his métier was to be what people thought he should be; the larger his audience, of course, the more he exaggerated the part he played. To obtain his audience, he sometimes had recourse to exhibitionist pranks. I have seen him throw himself into a ditch and roll over and over in it; bite pieces out of glasses; rip people's clothes; and at least once he went up to a group of strangers in a pub and said, 'Do you realize I am a famous poet?' The pub was his favourite stage for the acting of his parts, and his favourite role was that of orator. Surrounded by an admiring group, he would hold forth for hours, often very amusingly; but the art of conversation, in which there is a free interchange of comments, opinions, arguments, anecdotes, was not for him.

The fetch 'Dylan' was part of the false deluding 'outside world', and his place in it was that of a young devil, unscrupulous (but understandably so), ruthless (but forgivable), a liar (but not expecting to be believed), a cheat (only in matters that didn't really count), and a cynic (how dull to be otherwise!) This was the part he set himself to play, and he played it convincingly. Described coldly on paper, the role sounds repulsive, but, in spite of this, Dylan was warmly accepted by almost everybody who met him. This was, I believe, only in a small degree due to his fame. His charm, ingenuousness and childlike air made his 'wickedness' acceptable, like the 'wickedness' of an infant. To give one example: in his middle thirties, he paid a visit to Prague. When I was there myself a few years later, I happened to find some people who had met him during that visit, and more than one of them said, 'Your friend was a very naughty *little boy* (chlapeček)'; there was no serious reproof in the tone of their voices.

The hidden Dylan was indignant if anyone lied to him. The play-acting Dylan prided himself on preferring the lie to the truth. One day he boasted about this to me. 'The lie is imaginatively exciting, while the truth is flat and tedious. The lie is particularly good when it is without a motive; then it is *pure.*' He gave as a simple example the occasion when, in answer to his mother's question 'Which pocket is your handkerchief in?' he answered, 'The left', knowing that it was in the right.

The Dylan I am speaking about particularly liked to parade his cynicism about money. It is well known that he was in money difficulties throughout his life, and that throughout his life and after his death he left a trail of bouncing cheques and unpaid debts. One morning when I was staying at the Boat House in Laugharne, the post brought him a letter from a close friend. He opened it in front of me, pulled out the pages, peered elaborately between them, shook the envelope upside down, and at last exclaimed impatiently, 'No money! What's the use of a letter from a friend without money in it?' This performance was meant to impress me with his cynicism, of course.

Dylan's signature on his cheques was in itself amusing. As his bank account became depleted and passed from the pale blue into the deeper and deeper red, so his signature became smaller and smaller, until, it seemed, an electron microscope would be needed to read it. One day, keeping a straight face, I suggested that he should use an ink that would vanish without trace after a fixed interval. Now Dylan had a touching faith in my abilities, and knew nothing about my Ovid *Metamorphoses* gaffe. With equal seriousness, he said: 'Yes. That's it. Could you invent such an ink?'

I must record here, without offering any explanation, the remarkable fact that Dylan never borrowed any money from me. I leave the reader to his own theories. There was, however, the matter of my first library. Of this remarkable collection I recovered about fifty books — among them, ironically, the first edition of Dibdin's *The Library Companion*. A few had been stolen, others dispersed or lost, but almost all had been turned into cash. I did not reproach Dylan, or feel like reproaching him. There were too many excuses in his favour, and too much had happened in the immediate past. Before the war, I myself had made one removal from place to place, and the books filled an extraordinary number of tea-crates. Dylan made several moves; it was quite impossible for him to pay for carting all the books with him. Again, at least a third of the library consisted of books in foreign languages which he could not read, while others, like my Sacred Books of the East, held no attraction for him. And in the meantime . . . in the meantime, men had had their heads blown off, been sent to gas chambers, had been maimed, tortured, driven mad. There was no room any more for my petty bibliomania; I was cured of it for good.

Dylan was not always consistent in keeping his hidden self and his play-acting self apart; when he was alone with me, or perhaps with some other very close friend, or with children, his manner would become perfectly natural, and his character would open up to the light. It will, I hope, be of interest to the reader to learn how Dylan appeared in the eyes of an eight-year-old child. I am quoting from an article written by my son Dylan when he was in the sixth form of the 'Old School':

I was only eight when Dylan Thomas died. In fact, my most vivid memory was of his death. My parents had been in constant communication with New York during his illness and, when we were informed of his death, the grief which enveloped our house was such that it created an immense impression on me. Although this, my most vivid memory, is one of sadness, the chief impression that I had of him was of kindness and humour.

He called our house his town house, while we referred to the Boat House at Laugharne as our country residence. He visited us frequently, and his visits were remarkable for unexpectedness and haste. I well remember this, because when he arrived once at our house at seven o'clock in the morning after an unbroken journey from New York, it was I who had to get out of bed to open the door for him. The result of a particularly hurried departure of his serves as a good example of the extent to which his humour coloured his life; for he left all his shirts behind in a drawer. On the next day we received the following telegram: 'For Pete's sake send my shirts, Love, Pete.' His bedroom, after each departure, was always littered with apple cores, half-finished packets of liquorice all-sorts, and paper-back detective novels, which he read incessantly. He was always ready to join in a game. I remember one particular backyard test match, involving myself, my father and D.T., in which he broke my bedroom window. I, in fear of being accused of this by my mother, committed the sin of telling on him.

My general impression was that his visits always heralded a period of laughing and scuffling. One of these sessions of mock fighting resulted in my biting his thumb as hard as I could. Snatching his hand away, he looked at me gravely and said, 'Dog doesn't bite dog.'

However these gifts of humour and frivolity were coupled with an extreme consideration and kindness, many instances of which I can recall. The action he took when I suffered a disease of the heel* is typical of this; for, when he next visited London after I had contracted this condition, in spite of the fact that he had very important business there, he devoted his time to enquiring about the specialists best qualified to treat my complaint. In the letter which we received from him, he listed these specialists and ended by writing: 'Of these, the last named is the top, Love, Bottom.'

Dylan Thomas was a very welcome guest, and so much a friend of the family that, when I was born, he became my godfather. When I was a small boy, my chief impression of him was of a man full of generosity, kindness, and humour.†

At this moment how much I envy the great Latin historians who with such assurance and skill could epitomize a character in a sentence occupying the space of a paragraph, with every

* Epiphysitis, from which young Dylan soon recovered completely.
† Dylan Jones, VIA Arts: *I remember Dylan Thomas*, in the Swansea Grammar School Magazine, Christmas, 1963. The text has been abbreviated.

clause nicely balanced, every adjective scrupulously chosen, every epigram unobtrusively inserted, the solemn weight of the whole maintained in perfect equilibrium. At the same time, quite apart from my lack of the necessary skill, I am not in full sympathy with the procedure itself. I don't mean that the method is not aesthetically satisfying; it is, highly so. I mean that it is artificial, and that at best it expresses only half-truths.

In that case, if we cannot establish what is 'good' and what is 'bad' in estimation of character, is it not possible to find some compromise? What about Eli Jenkins's line in *Under Milk Wood*: 'We are not wholly bad or good'? No, it won't do. In my opinion, this utterance of the worthy Reverend is highly deceptive. It is full of trickery. I have no doubt about Dylan's attitude towards people like Eli Jenkins; he loved them, just as he loved my father, who was similar in many respects. But Eli is simply a character in a play. When he writes, he writes pastiche, with echoes from Dyer's *Grongar Hill*; when he expresses an opinion, it is his own, not Dylan's. It would be typical of such a man to regard ethical values two dimensionally, with the good in one direction, the bad at right angles to it, and a proposition like 'We are not wholly bad or good' represented by a diagonal drawn across a flat area. Eli's affirmation conceals sly ridicule of the whole concept of character as a gradation of white, innumerable greys, and black. Dylan has a similar aim in speaking of 'the good bad boys', a phrase everyone understands without quite knowing why.*

The 'flat' characterization in some histories and some fiction is excusable, of course; it has a satisfying finality and may serve a purpose. But, manifestly, it fails to correspond with truth and leaves the reader no imaginative scope, no room for wondering and questioning. When the book is closed, the characters are 'filed away' and forgotten. It is not like this with Hamlet or Tolstoy's Pierre or with any real person. Introspection suggests

---

* When I put to Dylan the conundrum: 'Which would you rather be, the scum of the cream or the cream of the scum?' he invariably replied (as Satan in *Paradise Lost* replied in other words), 'The cream of the scum.'

that beneath every layer there is another that shifts to reveal yet another layer; no point of stillness can be found where one can say, 'Here I stand.'

All this is obvious, perhaps trite; but I must say the obvious and the trite in order to explain why I shirk trying to reach any 'conclusion' about Dylan's character. As far as I am concerned, his character remains infinitely 'open', and I leave the reader to the infinite number of questions about it he may choose to ask himself.

There is a guessing game to do with the imaginary later careers of artists who have died young. What poems would Keats have written? What pieces would Schubert have composed? What pictures would Giorgione have painted? As far as I am concerned, enthralling as the game is, it remains a game, and has corresponding status. In this book I have deliberately avoided discussing Dylan's work, and the question, 'What would he have written if he had lived?' is ruled out on at least two counts: its irrelevance and its triviality. The question, 'Is it conceivable that he could have lived longer?' is of a different kind.

I have already suggested, obscurely perhaps, that there was a dichotomy in Dylan's character, at first deliberately created, then widening perhaps beyond his control. I cannot imagine how these two parts of his personality could be integrated and survive as one. When plus and minus meet, matter and anti-matter, the result is zero, annihilation. It seems to me that whatever the cause of Dylan's death, it had to happen when it did. Perhaps I am some kind of fatalist. I believe that the temporary individual, a segment of the shared consciousness of beings, a closed curve beginning from a point, must follow its characteristic course to a point determined from the first by its form; it can go nowhere else and no further, like a ball thrown into the air. For Dylan, the end was implicit in the beginning; nothing was possible except the course his life pursued, nothing possible beyond his predestined end. Belief in the Principle of Order leads to this, and no other conclusion.

116